PROTESTANT HOUR CLASSICS

PROTESTANT HOUR
CLASSICS

John R. Claypool
Robert E. Goodrich, Jr.
John A. Redhead, Jr.
Edmund Steimle
and others

ABINGDON PRESS
Nashville

PROTESTANT HOUR CLASSICS

This book is printed on recycled, acid-free paper.

Library of Congress Cataloging-in-Publication Data

Protestant hour classics / John Claypool . . . [et al.].
   p. cm.
Sermons delivered on the Protestant hour radio broadcast,
   1953–1988.
ISBN 0-687-34377-1 (alk. paper)
   1. Sermons, American. 2. Protestant churches—Sermons.
  I. Claypool, John. II. Protestant hour (Radio program)
  BX4815.P73   1992
  252—dc20   92-12752
                                             CIP

Grateful acknowledgment is made for use of excerpts from the following:

From the Revised Standard Version of the Bible, copyright © 1946, 1952,
1971 by the Division of Christian Education of the National Council of
Churches of Christ in the U.S.A. Used by permission.

From *The New Testament in Modern English, Revised Edition,* trans. J. B.
Phillips (Macmillan, 1972). Copyright © J. B. Phillips, 1958, 1959, 1960,
1972.

From the Authorized or King James Version of the Bible.

MANUFACTURED IN THE UNITED STATES OF AMERICA

PREFACE

The Protestant Hour is now a venerable institution. Throughout its forty-seven years of uninterrupted broadcasting, millions of listeners have tuned in to this program each week. Many thousands have requested the printed sermon copies for personal reading.

Since the first broadcast in 1945, listeners have had an opportunity to hear 465 individual speakers on 2,500 half-hour broadcasts. The program exposes listeners to a cross section of Protestantism, a wide range of theology, and great sacred anthems, hymns, and familiar music.

Through its interdenominational framework, a cooperative effort of the Episcopal Radio and Television Foundation, the Evangelical Lutheran Church in America, the Presbyterian Church (USA), and The United Methodist Church, *The Protestant Hour* continues among the largest and longest running religious radio programs available.

As responsible producers we are always stretching to provide fresh programming for our audience. Occasionally we see a benefit in rebroadcasting some of the memorable programs of the past.

In the archives of the Protestant Radio and Television Center, where *The Protestant Hour* is produced and distributed, is perhaps the richest treasure in Protestant preaching. It behooves us to share some of it before moving on to new material. Thus the "Classics," selected programs that stand out in the historical perspective of *The Protestant Hour.*

Webster defines classic as "of the highest class . . . fitting to serve as a model . . . a standard of excellence." Hence, our motive for the title "Classics" for this twelve-week series. Programs have been selected from the 50s, 60s, 70s, and 80s that, either individually or as part of a series, appear to "stand out" in form and content. Many other speakers and programs stand in the "Classic" tradition. We wish all of them could have been selected. Limited to twelve, however, our selection was made with the best intentions.

The messages from *The Protestant Hour* broadcasts that are printed in this book are for you: They are voices from the past, yet they are as powerful and relevant today as the moment they were originally presented. Our hope is that you will find in these messages a strengthened faith, inspiration, comfort, and most of all, enrichment in the gospel Word.

William W. Horlock, President
Protestant Radio and Television Center

CONTENTS

1.

God Is an Amateur

John R. Claypool

At the time he delivered The Protestant Hour *sermons, John R. Claypool was rector of St. Luke's Episcopal Church in Birmingham, Alabama.*

The year was 1988 . . . the Reagan era was coming to a close. . . . Party hopefuls Dukakis and Bush fought hard for election to the highest seat in the nation. In November, George Bush emerged the victor with 58 percent of the nation's vote.

Environmental problems made headlines . . . a huge hole in the ozone layer of the atmosphere, medical waste on beaches in the Northeast, massive forest fires out West, oil spills on the Ohio River, and two trapped gray whales off the northern coast of Alaska.

It was not a very good year for several newsmakers . . . Attorney General Edwin Meese resigned over alleged conflict of interest. Arizona governor Mecham was removed from office for obstructing justice. And several members of the Hunt family were convicted of conspiring to corner the silver market.

Jimmy Swaggart was defrocked by the Assemblies of God Church, the shroud of Turin was proved not to be the burial shroud of Christ, and Russia celebrated 1,000 years of Christianity.

Amateurs made headlines in 1988 as 13,000 amateur athletes gathered in Seoul, South Korea, for the running of the 24th Olympic Games.

✦ ✦ ✦

Words are like little children. They are always in motion and almost never still for long. For example, back in 1675, just nine years after the terrible London fire had devastated so much of that city, Sir Christopher Wren laid the cornerstone of what was to be his most ambitious undertaking—the rebuilding of St. Paul's Cathedral. He worked on the project for more than thirty-five years, and the experts say he poured more of his genius into this edifice than any other building ever designed. When the project was finally completed, and Sir Christopher himself was a very old man, he personally conducted the then reigning monarch, Queen Anne, on an extensive tour through the whole building. When it was over, he waited with bated breath for her reactions. In typical British terseness, she used three adjectives to sum up her feelings: "It is awful, it is artificial, it is amusing."

Can you imagine how the architect must have felt when the one person whose opinion he valued the most described the "magnum opus" of his life in this way? However, a biographer says that on hearing these words Sir Christopher let out an audible sigh of relief, sank to his knees, and thanked her majesty for her graciousness. How could such a reaction be possible? The answer lies in this fact—that words are always in motion and never stand still. For you see, back in 1710, the word "awful" meant "awe-inspiring," the word "artificial" meant "artistic," and the word "amusing" meant "amazing." I repeat, words like little children are always changing, which, incidentally, is why we have to continue to retranslate our scriptures and reformulate our liturgies and rituals. Words like everything else participate in an existence where the only thing that does not change is the fact of change itself.

And what has happened to words like "awful" and "artificial" and "amusing" has also happened to another English word, the term "amateur." As we use it in today's parlance, it stands for a person of limited competence. An amateur is the opposite of a professional, and the implication of the word is that such a person does not work with much skill and may even be something of a bumbler. However, this was not the case originally. Our English word "amateur" comes from the Latin root *amour,* which is the verb for "love." In its original intent, an "amateur" was a person who did whatever she or he did "for the love of it"; that is, their motivation came from within and not from without. An "amateur" was not paid to do something, nor coerced by any external force. The reason for such a person's act was positive intent. Here were folk who did what they did for the sheer joy of it.

In its original sense, then, one could go so far as to describe God as an amateur; in fact, this is precisely the import of the first chapter of Genesis. If you read those lyric lines as the inspired poetry they were meant to be, the image comes through of a Mystery who has life in itself and is desirous to share that life with others. You can almost hear God saying to God's self, "This aliveness that I'm enjoying, this wonderful power to be and to do—it is simply too wonderful to keep to myself. I want others to taste something of this ecstasy. I want the delight of aliveness to be a shared experience." Therefore, we watch in Genesis as this primal Generosity begins to act. Out of all the things God could have done, the Holy One freely decides to create. There is no hint of coercion, of external motivation here. Next, this One proceeds to carry out skillfully this intent to share, and it comes to a climax in the refrain that echoes through the whole chapter. "And God looked on what God had created and said, 'It is good, it is good, it is very, very good.'" The Hebrew image here is that of a little child having constructed something and then bringing in another to view it. Jumping up and down with delight, rubbing their hands together excitedly, they exclaim: "Isn't it grand, isn't it wonderful? Look what I have brought into being." All of this, of course, is precisely what lies behind the original meaning of this word "amateur." Here is One who freely selects an option out of all the possibilities, who effectively brings that potentiality into being, and then finds abundant delight in reflecting on all of it. In our modern usage, to call God "an amateur" might sound like a slight, but in the original sense, it gives us a glimpse into the very heart of the Eternal and helps us see that everything that exists in our world goes back to a Generosity that acted as it did for the sheer joy of it.

And this particular vision of God has practical relevance for each one of us, because the same book of Genesis goes on to affirm that we humans are made in the image of the Great Amateur; that is, we come to the fullness of our potential when we understand ourselves as having the same capacity to choose freely among many options, to act creatively on something that we want to do, and then to experience the delight that comes from such a way of life. The possibility of being an amateur is within the reach of every one of us, and I believe that the idea of the amateur best explains what it is we were meant to be.

I felt this would be a good note to sound on this particular weekend when our nation is celebrating Labor Day and giving specific thought to that part of our lives called "work." For many people, I am afraid that the

12

idea of their labor being that of "an amateur" is rather farfetched. There are many who feel the only possibility for this kind of experience lies outside their work. Their hobbies and avocations may have the characteristics of amateurism, but the thing they do to earn their livelihood does not. I do not want to be naive here; at the same time, however, I raise the possibility that if we were daring and imaginative enough and really believed that being an amateur is the essence of our true identity, there would be ways of asking ourselves, What do I really want to do? What are my best characteristics? What brings me the greatest delight of soul? And then we could begin to search for a way to make even our labor an expression of true amateurism. Such a quest may take lots of asking, and seeking, and knocking, much searching and experimenting and risk-taking, but the possibility of being what God is, namely "an amateur," exists for every one of us.

There is a wonderful old parable about a Jewish man named Isaac, son of Yeckel. His family had lived for generations in Cracow, Poland, and they had always been very poor. Isaac kept having a vivid dream that took place in Prague, Czechoslovakia. Isaac was told that if he would dig at a certain place under a bridge, he would find there immense treasure that would make him rich for the rest of his life. Finally, to the great dismay of his more practical family members, he announced that he was going to journey to Prague to test the reality of this beckoning. His contemporaries thought him crazy, but he set out nonetheless. He worked his way carefully across the center of Europe and finally reached Prague, where he had never been before, only to find it exactly as he had visualized it in his dreams. He went right to the bridge under which he

13

was to dig and with great excitement began to excavate. Suddenly, however, he felt a hand on his shoulder. It was a policeman saying, "This is public property. You are defacing it. You are under arrest." He was taken to a police station where an inspector began to interrogate him. Poor Isaac was so frightened that he did not know what to do but tell the truth about his dream. With that, the inspector laid back his head and laughed, and said, "You foolish dreamer. Don't you know there is nothing to these night fantasies?" He said, "Why, I myself have been having a dream of late. It was that if I would go to a village in Poland called Cracow, wherever that is, and go to the house of one Isaac, son of Yeckel, whoever that might be, and go into his kitchen and dig under his stove—there I would find a treasure to make me rich for the rest of my life. But would I not look foolish if I were to leave my good job here and go way off to Poland on such a wild goose chase?" With that he cuffed Isaac across the cheek and said, "Grow up, foolish dreamer, become a man, do something practical," and with that he threw him out of the police station. But Isaac, although harshly treated, was by no means depressed. He made his way back to Cracow, went to his own house, and into his own kitchen, dug under his own stove and there found the treasure that did in fact make him rich.

Here is the hope—that if we will listen carefully to our dreams, follow those beckonings of the heart—rather than spending all our energies on the speculative question "why?" we can begin to sift through the wreckage, pick up the pieces, and see what can be made of what is left, not because we understand it all, but because our very breath is a sign to us that we are still accompanied by the Lord of life. That One still wants us to be; therefore, we have a future in spite of all the losses of the past. Buechner says that when this gift of companionship became clear to Job, everything began to look different. He was like a man who asked for a crust and wound up being given the whole loaf. It is a possibility open to every one of us in the deepest and darkest places of our lives.

You are still breathing, aren't you? Take hope, take hope!

2.

A Divine Directive

Raymond D. Wood

At the time he delivered The Protestant Hour *sermons, Raymond D. Wood was pastor of the Lutheran Church of the Ascension in Savannah, Georgia.*

The year was 1953, a year of celebration. Jonas Salk was testing a vaccine to prevent polio. John and Jackie Kennedy tied the knot in a storybook wedding. Casey Stengel took the Yankees to their fifth World Series. And Lt. Col. Jacqueline Cochran became the first woman to break the sound barrier.

Then there was the entertainment side. People lined theaters to see a young actor named Burt Lancaster star in *From Here to Eternity*. Americans tuned in their T.V. sets to see the All American family, "Ozzie and Harriet," and one of the hit songs was "How Much Is That Doggie in the Window?"

Internationally, Queen Elizabeth II was crowned and Sir Edmund Hillary reached the top of Mount Everest. The Korean War came to an end and Soviet leader Stalin died.

The year 1953 had its fears. Americans felt the threat of Communism from the outside as well as from within. The Cold War had taken a new turn. Russian Premier Malenkov announced the USSR had a hydrogen bomb. Russian tanks crushed a labor revolt in East Berlin. At home 35,000 teachers in New York were issued a pamphlet about the dangers of Communist conspirators in schools. In November of 1953, Senator McCarthy went on national television to accuse Harry Truman of fostering Communism.

Jesus answered and said unto them, "Go and shew John again those things which ye do hear and see: The blind receive their sight, and the lame walk, the lepers are cleansed, and the deaf hear, the dead are raised up, and the poor have the gospel preached to them."

(Matt. 11:4-5)

When John the Baptist was in prison, he sent two of his disciples to Jesus asking, "Art thou he that should come?" John wanted to know beyond all doubt if Jesus were the promised Messiah or not. I can imagine his disciples putting the question quite bluntly: "Jesus of Nazareth, are you the Christ? The Son of God? The Savior of the world?"

Men are still questioning Jesus like that. They want to know if the Christ of Christmas is really the Christ of God. They listen to the prophets who foretold his coming, and then they look into Bethlehem's manger and wonder: Is that little baby there the sinner's Savior? They read the Bible and ask if it is true. They go to church and wonder if that is of Christ's making. They look at their sins and then at the cross and ask if there they find forgiveness. Perhaps you are asking that, too. If you are, it is important that you have the right answer.

Upon your knowledge of this truth hangs all eternity for you, and how and where you will spend it. If Jesus is not the promised Messiah, if his Word is not true, "then is our preaching vain, and your faith is also vain," and we who have put our trust in him "are of all men most miserable." And "they also which are fallen asleep in Christ are perished." So declares Paul in I Corinthians 15. But, if Jesus is the Son of God, then in him is salvation for everyone that believeth. Such is Christ's own promise: "Whosoever believeth in him should not perish, but have everlasting life." John's question, then, is a vital one. Isn't it? "Art thou he that should come?"

What is the answer? Jesus did not say yes or no when asked about his messiahship. Instead, he did what was more convincing. He did what the prophets had said that the Son of God would do. He did what only the Son of God could do. He gave sight to blinded eyes. He lifted up the lame. Lepers who came to him went away healed. Ears once stopped were made to hear again. Even the dead were raised to life once more. And what is sweeter still, he preached the gospel of love and life and health and happiness to the poor, who had known so little of it before. Jesus showed himself to be the Messiah.

After showing his inquirers all these things, Jesus then said, "Go and shew John again those things which ye do hear and see: The blind receive their sight, and the lame walk, the lepers are cleansed, and the deaf hear, the dead are raised up, and the poor have the gospel preached to them."

"Go and shew John," he said.

That is a directive, a divine directive, a command of Christ. "Go and show John." As a Navy shipboard chaplain in the Pacific during World War II, I learned that naval directives are not to be questioned. They are orders to be obeyed. As a soldier of the cross I have learned that even so are the commands of Christ. The disciples of John learned that also. Therefore, they went as Jesus directed them. Now we must go, for we, too, have heard and seen wonderful things in the fellowship of the Lord. Acts 10:39 describes us who have walked with the Master as "witnesses of all things which he did." We have witnessed that in Christ, which John's disciples knew nothing about. They saw the miracles of Jesus and they heard the gospel preached by him, but those who came after them saw the Christ upon his cross, and some heard his words from the cross, and others saw him on the Resurrection side of the cross and even witnessed his ascension into heaven as the victor over the cross. And "we are witnesses of all these things which he did." Therefore, we have much more to "show John" than did those earlier messengers. And so we must go. We must "go and show John those things."

Other versions of our text translate it "Go and *tell* John." The church must do more than "tell." We must "show" John what great things Jesus has done for us and said to us. By living our confession we must show John what the Master means to us. Every John, like the poet, would "rather see a sermon than to hear one any day."

John the Baptist needed to be shown. He was in doubt about Jesus. That is what prompted his question. His were honest doubts to be sure, but they were doubts just the same. They were doubts growing out of the troubles that had beset him. Out in the sunshine of the wilderness, John had been very sure of Jesus. On Jordan's banks he had pointed Jesus out as the Promised One, "the Lamb of God" who would take away the sins of the world. But now John was not sure of Jesus at all. Now John was in prison for preaching the truth, and there in the darkness of that dungeon his faith had grown dim.

That often happens to people in times of trouble. As long as the sun is shining there is no doubt at all in their

19

minds about the goodness of God. But when the skies become cloudy, sometimes doubts crowd in. When some calamity comes, some just stop believing the Bible sentence "God is love." "If God is love," they say, "and if Jesus is the Son of God, why does he leave John to languish in prison while evil men like Herod go free? Why doesn't he fling open the dungeon door and break the prisoner's chain?" Perhaps such questions have been yours in the hour of trial.

"If God is love, why did he make me as I am?" asked a young woman whose body was crippled and whose life was one of stress and strain. A loved one answered, and wisely, "He hasn't made you yet, my dear. He is making you now."

Nowhere does God promise those who love him exemption from suffering or sorrow or disease or death. But everywhere his promise is that the faithful will rise above their afflictions and march from victory unto victory though they live in the presence of pain. He even uses affliction to make his own what they ought to be. That, I think, is what David meant when he said in Psalm 119:71, "It is good for me that I have been afflicted." The good of faith is not that it removes obstacles. The good of faith is that it enables the faithful to surmount them.

There in prison John the Baptist was about to go down in defeat. His doubts were that real. But he didn't remain a doubter. He took his doubts to Jesus and left them there. That is always the way to deal with doubts. Take them to Jesus, not to his enemies or even to yours. Take them to Jesus. Take them to him on your knees in prayer. Prayer clears away clouds as nothing else can. Examine your fears in the light of the Holy Bible. This is a good day to do that. This is Universal Bible Sunday, a day that opens the Bible to us as God's blessed Book of Hope. Examine your fears in the light of God's Word. Take your questions to church with you. Many have done that and had them replaced with certainty. When John the Baptist was shown what his disciples had heard and seen, his doubts disappeared and he was on the right road again.

There are multitudes of others waiting to be shown what great things God can do through his Son, our Savior, Jesus Christ. The faith of some is failing for fear. For others it is want and worry and weakness darkening their days. The command of Christ is "Go and show John." If you have heard and seen the wonders of his grace, won't you go? I beg you, friend, "Go and shew John again those things which ye do hear and see." Go and show him again and again, if need be. You will find this doubter in every prison. This questioning one is in our hospitals, too. You may find him in that sickroom in the next block, or beside an open casket somewhere. That may be "John" working on the same farm with you, in the same office with you, or in the store buying something from you and hoping to see something in you that will relieve him of his doubts. If you know the truth about Jesus, I beg you to "Go and show John."

If you don't know Jesus, then in compliance with his divine directive I come to show you what he means to me. If you are not sure of Jesus, I want to show you what I have heard and seen in his service. As one who loves God's Word I hear him speaking to me through the Bible "as never man spake." I listen and in spite of my discouragements my heart grows warm in me and beats high with hope. If you are not sure of Jesus, I ask you to listen to his Word. On this Universal Bible Sunday, resolve that day by day you will read the Bible, and

21

let the Lord speak to you from its sacred pages. In the sound of his voice my fears fade. I believe his Word will do the same for you. I believe it because I have seen it do as much for many. One of them was a Marine sergeant who was aboard my ship for the Easter Day invasion of Okinawa in 1945.

He was a big fellow, that Marine, standing there in the door of my shipboard office that night before Easter. "Can you spare a minute?" he asked. Of course I could. That is why the chaplain is there. Very soon that young man was telling me how deeply afraid he was of all that was threatening him. "Chaplain," he said, "we'll be hitting the beach again tomorrow, and I've got a feeling that I won't be coming back. This will be the third landing for me. I came through the other two all right, but this time I've got a hunch I'm going to get it. And I don't mind telling you, I'm plenty scared." With trembling lips, that Marine asked me about death, and with a prayer in my heart I answered him as clearly and as faithfully as I could.

Then I said, "You have no need to fear death. For one who believes in Jesus, death is simply passing from this life to that which is better. You have no need to fear death, if you believe in Jesus."

"Well," he said, "I'm not too sure that I do believe. If I do, I know my faith isn't what it ought to be." Then he added, "I guess that's why I'm so afraid to die."

We talked a little longer, and then, after our prayer, I handed him a pocket Testament with the Psalms in the back. I had marked the fourteenth chapter of John: "Let not your heart be troubled . . . ," and the twenty-third psalm: "Though I walk through the valley of the shadow of death, I will fear no evil: for thou art with me; thy rod and thy staff they comfort me." He put the little book in his pocket and left. Others came and still others with their cares until general quarters sounded just before daybreak.

When the Marines were going over the side of the ship at dawn and down into the landing craft, which would take them to the enemy beach, I stood by wishing them well on their way. Among the first to go over the side was my Marine sergeant friend. He looked at me and smiled, patted his pocket where he carried the New Testament I had given him, and said, "It's all right now, Chaplain. I'm not scared anymore." And he wasn't. He had spent the night with God's Word.

I could show you many like that young man, filled with fear at first, then calm with confidence after an hour of prayer and spending a while with God's Word. If you are afraid of something or for someone and your fears have left you in doubt, I should like to show you these things wrought by Christ in others, things which I have heard and seen: the weak strengthened, the fallen lifted, and the dying filled with hope. If you are a modern "John," fearful in the face of these threatening times and quailing before the possibilities of the hostilities which persist in this atomic age, and if you doubt Christ's power to help, let me show you this sentence which he spoke: "All power is given unto me . . . and, lo, I am with you."

If you have known the hurt of sin, I should like to show you the sin-wrecked lives I have seen Jesus rebuild by his grace. I should like to assure you that "he is able also to save them to the uttermost that come unto God by him." If you are pinched by pain or pressed by problems and you wonder if Christ cares, I come to you with his peace promising "Come unto me, all ye that labour and are heavy laden, and I will give you rest." If it is death that is threatening you or some loved one and disturbing you with doubt, let me show you Jesus raising Lazarus from the dead and the daughter of Jairus, and the widow's son at Nain; and let me read to you this sacred sentence, which fell from the Savior's lips: "I am the resurrection, and the life: he that believeth in me, though he were dead, yet shall he live."

I come to you with these precious promises because Jesus said, "Go and shew John again those things which ye do hear and see." Having heard and seen them I just had to show them to you. When John the Baptist was shown them he knew that Jesus was the Christ, the Son of God, the Messiah and the Savior of the world. Now you have heard and seen them, too. I pray that what you have heard and seen will do as much for you.

The peace of God, which passeth all understanding, keep your hearts and minds through Christ Jesus.

3.

What Does God Look Like?

Robert E. Goodrich, Jr.

At the time he delivered The Protestant Hour *sermons, Robert E. Goodrich, Jr., was pastor of First Methodist Church in Dallas, Texas.*

The year was 1963 . . . Pope John XXIII died and Paul VI was elected. The Soviet Union sent a woman into space. The Vietnam conflict became more intense. Moviegoers raved over *The Birds, Tom Jones,* and *Dr. Strangelove.* Peter, Paul, and Mary sang "Puff, the Magic Dragon" and "Blowin' in the Wind" as American youth tuned them in on the radio.

The biggest story of 1963 was the assassination of President John F. Kennedy. The president was shot on the streets of Dallas in his open limousine. Lee Harvey Oswald was arrested hours later.

Dr. Martin Luther King addressed 200,000 persons in Washington with his famous "I Have a Dream" speech. Civil rights leader Medgar Evers was assassinated. A bomb exploded in a Birmingham, Alabama, church, killing four girls. Civil rights struggles dominated the headlines of our nation's news.

In 1963 black people were being mentally and physically abused. They raised their hands high and cried for civil rights.

And where were the churches? Dr. Eugene Carson Blake of the United Presbyterian Church, along with fellow clergy, addressed a crowd in a Baltimore amusement park that forbade black attendance. Dr. Blake and his fellow church leaders gathered together with a simple biblical idea, that all people, regardless of race, are created in the image of God. That leaves us with one big question: What does God look like?

On a visit to Russia, a friend of mine was talking with a young woman bus driver. "I understand that in America nearly everybody believes in God," she said. He answered that about 90 percent of the people claim to believe in him. The young woman thought for a moment and then asked, "Tell me, what does your God look like?"

She was asking a crucial question for all of us. What does he look like . . . in character? What is the shape of his love, his goodness, his judgment?

Many persons hold a picture of God in their hearts, which makes me wonder how on earth they could ever love him, or even respect him. When tragedy comes, for example, they immediately begin to ask, Why did God do this to me? Why did he take my husband? We had so many plans and dreams! Why did he send this lingering illness upon my child?

I was on the Texas coast about twelve months after hurricane Carla had wrought her terrible destruction. There were rows of homes still so water-damaged that their owners had not been able to return to them. And though a year had passed, more than once I heard the question "Why do you think God sent this upon us? We must have been doing something terribly wrong." What does God look like for them?

A young man in a hospital wrote to his pastor a letter, which included these sentences: "For months I have been on this bed with time to think. Tell me, sir, in view of the facts of life, have I any reason to love God? I believe some God exists but be good enough to tell me why I should love him."

So everywhere there are persons who don't bother with the church because frankly they do not like the kind of God whom they imagine is worshiped in the church. They carry a picture of him fashioned from hearsay, or from fragmentary experiences remembered from Sunday school days, or from the words of some traveling revivalist in other years. They would say to us, "We don't want to believe in your God! We have outgrown your childish ideas of a sort of super-man sitting out on the rim of the universe somewhere, running things like a king, pulling the strings on life so that everybody's real name would be Punch and Judy! Nor do we like the idea that from up there somewhere he sends sorrow and suffering and pain upon persons in order to get even with them or to punish them or to test their faith. And furthermore, we don't like your ridiculous idea of a glorified private-eye always watching us so that he can put down a checkmark or a gold star by our name in his big black book!"

To be sure this composite picture sounds overdrawn, and yet the various ideas out of which it is made are present all around us. But what does God really look like?

Perhaps it is foolish to try to deal with such a subject within the space of these few minutes, but we can at least make a beginning. Granted that it is impossible for the finite mind to encompass the infinite: We cannot completely picture him or express him in human language or thought. But we can have the spirit of the man who said to Jesus, "Lord, I believe; help thou mine unbelief." There is much beyond our power of understanding or comprehension, but on the other hand, there are surely some things we can grasp. And we can make an effort to bring into sharper focus a picture of the God of the Christian faith as seen in the revelation of Jesus Christ. Lord, I believe; help thou mine unbelief!

Let's begin with that idea that God is a super-king, a manlike dictator, sitting off somewhere on the rim of the universe pulling the strings of life.

In a paper on religion, a college student described her struggle with such a picture. She said that as a child in church, she used to be fascinated with the angels in the stained-glass windows. She would imagine that she could see a great throne-room with the soft, billowy clouds for the floor and the bright blue sky for the ceiling. Seated down at one end of the room in a huge chair was a bewhiskered old gentleman, in the fashion of a patriarch of Israel, who she was sure was God. In and out of the room floated pink and blue and lavender angels. "But one day," she concluded, "I grew out of my visions in pastels and found myself left with nothing at all . . . nothing."

This is the final and inevitable result of trying to believe in a manlike God. And yet most of us began as children with a picture of him that was a strange blend of Father Time and Santa Claus and Daddy! As we grew in wisdom and understanding, however, we put away childish things and have come to believe with Jesus Christ that "God is a Spirit, and they that worship him must worship him in spirit and in truth." He is not a God who is just up there, he is down here; he is not just out there, he is in here. We believe he is everywhere present, always.

When a friend of mine asked his little son to say

28

grace at the table, he came forth with these words: "God is good, God is great, clear across the Lone Star state." But you and I know that he must be a God who is not limited to these fifty states, or to this continent, or even to this earth. We believe that he is a Spirit, always near, everywhere present, no matter where we go.

But if this is what he looks like, why do we go on referring to him as having manlike qualities? Why do we talk of "the everlasting arms," or of "walking with him, talking with him"? Why do we speak of "the eyes of God" or the "hand of God"?

We do this because, for one thing, we are hopelessly limited to the language of our experience. In a sense we are earthbound in our efforts to express that which reaches far beyond the earth.

But a more important reason is that human personality is the highest that we know. Within the range of our knowledge, it alone can plan and create and love and sacrifice. And I think we reason correctly when we conclude that surely God is more like a man than like a jellyfish, or a chair, or a tree. To picture God in the terms of our experience is not to limit him to human nature. It is rather to say, "I believe; help thou mine unbelief."

Furthermore, we are persuaded that we can often see him reflected in human personality. After all, the word became flesh and dwelt among us! Surely the Incarnation was a part of the eternal revelation.

A college sophomore—which, as you know, is the wisest of all men—came home for the Christmas holidays loaded with arguments with which to puncture the religious faith of his parents. These arguments had been gleaned from his first acquaintance with biology and geology on the college level. Now he could hardly wait to launch his attack. Sitting in front of the fire after din-ner, waiting for an opening, he looked at his mother, noting the deep lines in her face and hands, which somehow recalled for him the personal battles she had fought and won through her faith. Then he turned toward his father, and something brought to his mind the memory of that habit which had nearly ruined their home; it had been conquered through faith. Suddenly, all of his arguments began to vanish in the presence of this witness to the power of faith expressed in human personalities. One could not argue with a living fact!

We will go on describing God in terms of human personality, even though we know that he is Christ-like, not manlike; even though we know that he is not up there but is down here, not out there but in here. God is a Spirit everywhere present, always.

Another element of that composite picture was the idea that God orders suffering and pain, paralysis, and even death upon persons just to get even with them or test their faith. Is this what he looks like?

In James Agee's novel *A Death in the Family,* the young husband is killed in a senseless one-car accident; a little bolt came loose and the car swerved off the highway. Later in the evening the brother of the new young widow came to be with her. As he entered the room his first comment was: "Now . . . what about that idiot God of yours!"

If God decrees and directs such tragedies, then the phrase would seem to fit. When a man does such a thing he is removed from society, put behind bars, or judged sick in mind and spirit. If on the one hand God loves us, and with the other hand afflicts us with such monstrous suffering, then he would be schizophrenic! It is not a criminal God but a Christ-like God in whom we believe!

This leaves questions, however, which someone might

put like this: "If he is a God of love who cares about us, then why does he allow such natural catastrophes as hurricanes, tornadoes, earthquakes, and the like, these things which are sometimes legally defined as 'acts of God'? They take a tragic toll; why does he allow them?"

Let's imagine that we possess the power to banish these things. But before we do it, perhaps we should remember that there is a relation between the tornado tearing the sky and the wheat which grows in the field, between a hurricane and a rose. They are all part of one great body of natural law. To make it impossible for an earthquake to happen might also make it impossible for grain to grow. Perhaps this is not only the best possible world; it may be the *only* possible world.

Conceivably our questioner might say, "All right, then, we'll keep natural law with its consequences: But if he loves us, why doesn't God banish sin? It would be such a wonderful world if there were no such thing as sin!"

Let's imagine that it is also within our power to banish the possibility of sin. But before we do it, perhaps we should consider that if we do away with the possibility of evil, we do away with the possibility of good. *Virtue* and *honor* and *nobility* would become words with no meaning. No wonder a young man in the midst of a discussion on this subject finally said, "I demand the right to be damned!" You see, the right to be saved and the right to be damned go together.

So now our questioner might agree that we do better to keep the possibility of sin. "But if God loves us," he would say, "couldn't he at least do away with pain? This is what spoils so much of life—headaches and backaches and toothaches . . . and heartaches with their own special kind of suffering! Why doesn't God banish pain?"

31

Once again, let's imagine that we have such power. We would banish pain from the world! But before we do away with its possibility, I have a newspaper clipping that puzzles me. It describes a little girl in a northern city who has already received this great blessing; she can feel no pain. Cut her, burn her, stick a pin in her, it would not matter; she has no capacity to feel pain. So is she called "blessed"? Well, strangely, the article describes her as a tragic case and tells how medical scientists are doing everything in their power to restore to this girl the capacity to feel pain! Strange? Not when we remember that the capacity to feel pain is the sign of sensitivity; no pain, no joy; no tears, no laughter; no sorrow, no rejoicing.

Then perhaps we do better to keep even this capacity to feel pain. This may be the only possible world in which men can become great in character, deep in sympathy and understanding, all so that they may become sons of God.

What does God look like? Please do not misunderstand. The point is that he does not arbitrarily send these tragedies upon us; they are within his will in the sense that, so far as we can see, without their possibility, our life in this world would not be possible. He does not send them; but if we do not shut him out, God will come with the tragedy or pain to help us to use them and not waste them. This is the pattern in which he used even the Cross.

A father whose daughter was stricken with polio told me that he thought it was one of the great things that had happened to their family. I asked him what on earth he meant by such a statement. He explained that there were several reasons. "For one thing, we are so proud of our daughter—the way she has handled this illness in her own spirit. And then," he continued, "We're grateful for the way in which our family has been drawn together in this experience; we have never been so close as a family. It is as if we have discovered each other. And third, we never guessed that we had so many friends here in the city; people who cared enough about us to send flowers and food and messages. And then, for the first time we really know what the Church and our faith really mean. I don't know what we would have done without them. And so . . . for these reasons we think polio is one of the great things that has happened in our family."

I could never believe God sent polio upon a child in order to teach a family these lessons, or to test their faith, or reveal it to them. But when that tragedy entered, they did not shut him out; and he helped them to use it and not waste it.

One other part of the composite picture is the concept of God as "heavenly private-eye," or as divine book-keeper, always watching so that he may put down some mark by our name in his big black book!

In my grandparents' home, there was a picture I despised as a child growing up. In the center of the large frame there was one great big eye. Arranged around this eye were the symbols of civilization: trucks and plows and tractors and engines and factories—all sorts of things. Even as a child I reasoned that this was some sort of a representation of God; that great big all-seeing eye. But, frankly, I simply didn't like the thought of a one-eyed God! But what I disliked most of all was the way in which . . . well, if I were to take a supply of dried leaves or coffee grounds or grapevine out behind the barn, and roll it up carefully in some tissue paper and put it in my mouth, then just as I would get the match up to light it . . . around the corner of the barn would come that terrible, terrible eye!

Some people imagine that this is the way God sees us; as an eye always out to catch us and condemn us. I do believe he sees us . . . however, not with an eye to condemn, but with an eye of love that never lets go of us. But never think that it is not a terrible thing to be loved like this! When we are loved, then everything we do is judged in the light of that love. Whenever I have an unworthy thought, or contemplate an ugly or evil deed, I do not suddenly think of a judgment day out in the future. I think of those who love me and believe in me. And I stand judged in the light of their love!

What does God look like? One who sees us, not with an eye to catch us and condemn us, but with an eye of love which never gives up, never lets go. Like a shepherd who watches over his sheep, like a father whose eyes keep searching the road for some sign of the prodigal coming home, a love like a mother's love.

A young man once came to me with the request that I write a letter to a little town up in New England to learn if his mother was still alive and living there. "I used to send her a card or a message on Mother's Day, but I haven't done it in a long time," he explained. "I don't even know if my Mother is still living. Would you find out for me? If she is still there, I'm going to send her a card this year."

Of course I would write the letter for him. I sent it by airmail the same afternoon. Within four days, I think, I had an answer. She was still at the same address. In her letter to me, this mother said, "So that is where that no-good son of ours is living. He violated every principle we had in our home. He's turned his back upon everything we have tried to do for him. He has disgraced our name. You tell that boy I never want to see him again . . . "

Do you think this is what that mother wrote? Then you don't know mothers. Instead, she said, "So that's where our boy is. How long would it take me to get to Texas from here? Tell him that we love him." A mother's love, you see, never gives up.

Like a shepherd; like a father; like a mother's love. So the love of God never gives us up, never lets go. And in the light of such a love are we judged.

What does God look like? This is the crucial question. Any picture we hold will be partial, incomplete; we cannot encompass the eternal. But we can measure our every thought of him by what we see in Jesus Christ. He is not up there but is down here; he is a Spirit everywhere present, always. Measuring by Christ, we know that God does not order suffering and send tragedy upon us; rather, when it enters our life, if we do not shut him out, he will come with it to help us use it and not waste it. Measuring by Christ, we know that he sees us not with an eye of condemnation, but with an eye of love that never lets go and waits the day when we may say at last:

> Just as I am, thy love unknown,
> Hath broken every barrier down;
> now, to be thine, yea, thine alone,
> O Lamb of God, I come, I come.

4.

The Problem of Unresolved Grief

Alexander M. McGeachy

At the time he delivered The Protestant Hour *sermons, Alexander M. McGeachy was pastor of West Raleigh Presbyterian Church in Raleigh, North Carolina.*

The year was 1983 . . . President Ronald Reagan ordered an invasion of Grenada. Benigno Aquino returned from exile to the Philippines and was promptly assassinated at the Manila airport. This sparked a revolution, which later toppled the Marcos Regime. And the Martin Luther King, Jr., holiday bill was signed into law.

The Presbyterian Church US and the Presbyterian Church USA completed their merger. The Roman Catholic bishops of the United States denounced nuclear war, and religious leaders gathered in Washington to urge Congress to ban genetic engineering.

From the entertainment side, Vanessa Williams was crowned the first black Miss America, and former President Gerald Ford made a cameo appearance on "Dynasty."

The year 1983 had its tragedies. Korean airlines flight 007 was shot down by the Soviets; 269 persons were killed. In Beirut, the United States embassy and a building used to house marines were bombed; the total loss was more than 255 persons. And we grieved over the loss of Alabama football coach Bear Bryant, Tennessee Williams, Gloria Swanson, Arthur Godfrey, boxer Jack Dempsey, and singer Karen Carpenter.

What is the best sermon ever preached on *The Protestant Hour?* Who can tell? With a history of more than fifty-two sermons a year and thirty-five years of broadcasting, there is no way we could pick one that we would say was best.

But though we cannot say which sermon was best, I can let you know the sermon that has had more requests for reprints than any other in the thirty-five years of broadcasting. That sermon was preached March 8, 1959, by Dr. John A. Redhead, Jr., and was entitled "The Problem of Grief." What that sermon did was to give people permission to grieve, to be sad, to mourn over the loss of a loved one. "Blessed are they who mourn," says Jesus in the Beatitudes, "for they shall be comforted." Christians who feel that it is not appropriate to grieve need to hear that, especially through mourning, we are able to find the peace and comfort that God has for us.

Now what this sermon will attempt to do is to build on that marvelous foundation of twenty-four years ago and to share with you some of the insights that have been learned since about grief and to speak to the issue I as a pastor see is still around. That issue is the problem of unresolved grief.

Let me state the issue of unresolved grief this way. People are learning that it is all right to grieve. Even men are showing their feelings, crying possibly at the time of a loss of love. We are discovering that mourning is not only good spiritual health, it is excellent mental health as well. The problem comes because it takes three years at least to get over a serious loss of the death of a loved one, and the world will only allow us to grieve for six months. Now the issue for you is that gap. What do you do with all those feelings of loss, sadness, confusion, loneliness, which you carry around in you when your family and friends around you do not seem to want to hear about it anymore? They want you to get back with it, into life.

Now before we look directly at the question, I feel it would be helpful to remind you of what seems to be universally accepted as the stages of grief. For when we have these right in front of us then we will be able to decide how to handle them.

Grief is our response to loss, any loss; the greater the loss, the greater the grief. We usually think of grief as coming from a death, the loss of a loved one, and there is certainly no greater loss than the loss by death of a loving partner, husband or wife, unless it's the loss of a child by its mother. But the feelings and response of grief are the same for any kind of loss. Divorce and the loss of a married partner, though both of you are still alive, can be a way of bringing grief reactions, and at such a time there is no one to bring in food and sustain us through the pain and loneliness. Loss of childhood can do the same. Grief is response to a loss, any loss.

And what is our response to those losses? Diane Henderson, a grief counselor in Raleigh, North Carolina, says there are seven distinct stages or steps that we must go through. First there is the shock and denial of the death. "Oh, my God, he is gone. I just can't believe it. I won't believe it. I will not believe that this has happened to me." In that first stage you feel very much like it's been a bad dream, a nightmare from which you cannot wake up. The next stage very simply is one of depression and deep sadness. You may seem to have a terrible case of the blues, in which everyone and everything around you may seem callous and bleak. Words of comfort appear hollow and cheap. No one feels as you now feel. In the third stage, you can move into anger. Anger at the loss, anger at the doctor for not doing enough, anger at God for taking away your loving partner. The fourth stage is one of confusion and bewilderment. There is so much to do, so many things to decide, and you cannot think straight and come to grips with life. Every decision seems like a mountain. And then there is the stage of guilt. You remember all the things you did not do for that person. "If only . . . " goes over and over again in your mind, "If only . . ." then they would still be alive and living here. Then comes the idealization stage, in which you close your realistic view of the one who has left you. Don't ever say anything bad about those who are gone is the principle here. A man once told me, "I want you to meet the perfect man. He's my wife's late first husband." And finally there comes at last an acceptance and a feeling of peace, a giving in to the inevitable. They are gone, yes; I do not like it, but I must go on. What must be must be, and so you do.

Now the problem of unresolved grief is this: We get stuck in one of those seven stages and cannot move through to acceptance of the inevitable and to peace. Jesus says in the Sermon on the Mount, "Blessed are those who mourn," as if to say "Congratulations" to those who can grieve or work through the sadness, work through the anger, work through the guilt, work through the idealization. For those are the people who can find acceptance and peace from the shock and trauma of loss.

After twenty-five years in the pastorate, it is my considered opinion that there is more behavior determined by unresolved grief than by any other single thing. I know people who are very blue, constantly down in the dumps, who will cry at the slightest thought of sadness and yet do not know why. My guess is that there is a loss in their past that they have not resolved. I know people as you do, who are always angry, who go through life with a chip on their shoulder, a bah humbug attitude about whatever is happening to them, and I wonder why they are caught in this anger stage. I know people as you do, who have a burden of guilt about everything and cannot be freed to live now because they are always feeling guilty about some person or place or thing in the past that they cannot shake off. I know people as you do, who cannot live fully in the town they are living in now because they keep saying how wonderful it was in the place that they have left. All of that arises from being caught in some stage of grief, but Jesus, from the mountain, says congratulations to those who can mourn and who can move on to the acceptance stage, for only as they are moving through the stages will they be able to find comfort.

Grief work, and it is surely work, is the ability to look very closely at what you are thinking and feeling and work through the strain, the pain, the loneliness of each stage, until you can move on to acceptance. Move from the loss and back into life. Jesus from the mountain says congratulations to those who can do this.

Before I mention some specific steps on how to work through grief, let me mention why it is hard for a person to move on. Grief has been described as the tension of wanting to go forward in life together with not wanting to leave the past. Even though that past may have been bad, we do not want change. We may feel that if we do move on we are acting out of selfishness and disrespect for the memory of the person we have lost.

Please let me change that right now and speak to you as the person who has gone on. Your loved one has now moved on. Yet, if our faith means anything we know that they are better off than they have ever been here on earth. You are not helping them at all by trying to hold on to them in memory and refusing to live. They want you to live. And to face tomorrow does not mean in any way that you did not love them fully then. Death may have ended their life, but it will never end your relationship. Congratulations, says Jesus from the mountain, to those who can work through that change and find acceptance and peace.

I am wondering if while listening to this sermon you have identified some part of your life or the life of someone you love caught in one of these stages of grief, unable to find life, and unable to move on in life's journey. To you and for those you love, let me mention three things that may help you work through the stages of grief. Let us hope that they will assist you in striving to reach to the next stage and ultimately assist you in finding the acceptance and peace God has for you.

First, and this suggestion may seem very simple, talk. Talk, talk, and more talk. Talk about the person you have lost. Talk about the friend who is now gone. Talk about the pet you used to have. If there is no one around who will listen, go to a person who is trained to listen, such as a pastor. If no one is available for free, go to someone that you have to pay, such as a professional therapist, who will listen and talk with you. Talk about what is on your mind and in your heart. Talk about it even if it seems silly to you. Talk about it when you do not sense the pattern, until the pattern becomes clear.

Second, if there is no one around at all to listen, or even in addition to one being around to listen, write down your thoughts and feelings. Begin a journal, which is much like a diary of feelings. Try to write without making judgments about what you are writing. Don't say to yourself, This is good or this is bad, or I should not be saying this about them. Write and let your feelings out, and if you will, let the poison out. Write a private letter to the person who is gone and say what you always wanted to say to that person and now don't seem to be able to. Write your own biography, saying where you are now and what is happening to you. As you listen to my voice what I am saying may seem very simple, even silly to you, but I can assure you that it works. It has worked for me and for many others that I have known very closely. Jesus from the mountain says, congratulations to you if you can do this, for then you will find peace and comfort.

Third, try to look for the positives. I mean not simply to cover up your unpleasant feelings but to see those feelings, those pains in a new way. What have you learned now about life because of this loss? I remember with gratitude what I learned about death and life working through the grief of my father's passing. Do you have a new skill? Did you learn to do something for yourself for the first time, such as writing a check or balancing the checkbook at the end of the month? Did you have to get a job? Do you now have to braid your daughter's hair because her mother is no longer with her? The word here is *reframing,* meaning to try looking at the painful parts in a new way. The essence of Christianity is that in death there is life. Jesus from the mountain says congratulations to those who can work through the pain, for they will find comfort.

In the death of Jesus on the cross, we have a horrible end to the perfect life. But the end of life is not the grave; it is Easter morning. And when you have suffered a loss, no matter how large or small, you go through the same pattern Jesus did. A part of you dies, yes, but another part of you can come alive. Jesus from the mountain says congratulations to those who can move through the loss, through that death so that a newer part may come to life.

Finally, let me say that though death may end a life, death can never end your relationship. The love that God gives us is stronger than the power of death and the grave, and though we will never see our loved ones alive in the same way we saw them before, or talk to them as we did or touch them as we did, the love that we had is that bridge that keeps us together and in some measure closer than we could have been when both of us were alive. Since that love holds us together now, it is a loving thing to move on. Your love does not die; it assists you and transforms you into a new understanding of life.

If you are caught in one of the stages of grief, I am very sorry, but there is help. Please remember this formula—you very well may need to grieve for three years or more. The world on the other hand may not want you to drop out for more than six months. So be good to yourself and patient with yourself. If you are willing to work through the pain, the sadness, the anger, acceptance can come. I can assure you that Jesus from the mountain is encouraging you, inviting you to begin now. New life and resurrection is ahead for you. Congratulations to you if you can find it.

5.

God Doesn't Need
Our Protection

Bennett J. Sims

At the time he delivered The Protestant Hour *sermons, Bennett J. Sims was associate dean at Virginia Theological Seminary in Alexandria, Virginia.*

The year was 1967, a year of war and of a changing society. Egypt and Israel clashed in the Six-Day War. China's cultural revolution caused tens of thousands of deaths. The civil war in Biafra killed thousands by starvation. And the race riot wars in the streets of the United States jolted large cities.

In 1967 world attention was focused on the war in Vietnam. President Lyndon Johnson increased troops by 45,000. The United States bombed Hanoi, and Americans were hotly divided over the conflict.

Protests against the war and the draft were nationwide. Fifty thousand persons marched on the Pentagon in a demonstration that turned to violence.

The year 1967 will be remembered for the emergence of the hippie. American youth broke from tradition. They spoke out against what they called "the Establishment." Hippie protests focused on institutions, the educational system, and religious organizations.

✦ ✦ ✦

Every now and then something comes through the language of the Gospels that gives Jesus the sparkle that I'm sure was there in the flesh-and-blood man. There is no accounting for his impact on men, women, and children apart from the radiant charm of a consummate human being. There is no direct laughter in the church's recollection of Jesus, but I cannot believe there was no laughter in people's experience of Jesus.

Perhaps the laughter is missing from the record because the crucifixion is the dominant event in the record—and there is no gaiety in that. But I do think I can hear laughter in the background of some of his sayings—not raucous guffaws, but the amusement of people who felt charmed and won to the truth by a man of good humor.

Take a saying like the one in Luke 6:41, but take it in language more appropriate to the figure he used, that is to say, current, conversational. This is the J. B. Phillips translation: "Why do you look at the speck of sawdust in your brother's eye and fail to notice the plank in your own? . . . You fraud, take the plank out of your own eye first and then you can see clearly to remove the speck out of your brother's eye."

When you put the truth this way, it probably doesn't make it any easier to practice, but it makes the meaning harder to miss and easier to hear. They must have smiled, many of them, to hear him speak the truth using a figure. This figure of speech is hyperbole—or overstatement for the sake of emphasis—which is one of the great forms of humor. The *New Yorker* magazine carried a cartoon awhile ago showing a middle-aged couple at a meal on their patio. Nearby, at the edge of the patio, was a grass hut in front of which a young woman knelt, wearing African dress and stirring a pot over an open fire. The caption read: "Gwendolyn, now that you're home from the Peace Corps, your mother and I feel it is time that you return to the ways of your people." This is overstatement of the common problem of reentry that everyone feels in returning to his country after a period of service elsewhere. Jesus used this technique of hyperbole many times.

Now, we may rightly think of Jesus as a humorist. If we cannot grant him this attribute, one necessary to any healthy, charming, charismatic man, then I would put it down as evidence of a particular plank in the church's eye.

I will say what I think the plank is in a minute, but first, as a teacher in a theological school, I visit many different churches for worship, big ones and little ones, and of many different denominations. All of them are very proper, the services well conducted, earnest. But for the most part, most of them convey no joy and almost no direct contact with the sounds and shape of the world in which we live. Something is missing that catches fire, the fire of hope and joy we long for.

Now, as to the plank that may be in our eyes as churches: It is the idea that we are in business to defend the reputation of God and protect his delicate sensibilities against offense by the naughty world. On the Washington Cathedral grounds last summer, a rock 'n' roll youth rally was rained out, so that the whole thing was moved inside the great Gothic building and several groups of musicians were placed here and there and played in turn. At first the young people only listened—3,000 of them—but then, caught up in the gaiety of the music and the moment, some began to dance. A picture appeared the next morning on the front page of the *Washington Post*. You can imagine that the Bishop of Washington had a sizable controversy on his hands!

Now this kind of unplanned, earthy exuberance before the altar of God raises some profound questions as to the meaning of real worship, how much it is intended to rise out of the reality of our lives. But I cannot believe the question as to the meaning of worship should be settled on the basis of our fear of offending God. Any God who would bless the monstrous din of sheephorn blasts loud enough to knock down the walls of Jericho is not offended by the sound of the Beatles or their kind.

What I am suggesting is that if in the church we behold the godlessness of the world and seek to pluck the dirt from the world's eyes, we had best take heed of the plank that may blind us to the activity and the presence of God in the world—in its music, in its momentum. If we hang on to the old words and formulas, hymns and liturgies of the church for fear of offending God with something new and earthy and human, then we are profoundly misguided. We are victims of a far more damaging heresy than rejecting the virgin birth or even the divinity of Christ—for what it means is that we have a god about as vigorous as a retired choir director in a nursing home. If we perpetuate archaisms in the church simply out of respect for God's dignity and reputation among men, then we have yet to believe that the Son of God was born of a peasant girl in a cowstall.

I am not suggesting that we abandon dignity or the overpowering sense of mystery, but only that so much of what is meaningful in our tradition has become stuffy, not majestic, has become hocus-pocus, as it were, to our young people and others, and not authentically mysterious. So much of the power to move men in their depths has fled the old forms and words and sounds. Maybe we do not do them well enough, or believe them well enough. Or maybe it is simply that the beauty and mystery and power and miracle of life reach us more readily in the great human things that happen in the world.

Do you know where I weep? In the movies and at the theater, where I see human courage and compassion confront the suffering and anguish and absurdity of life. I weep at the Lincoln Memorial to read again the Second Inaugural and be gripped anew by the dignity of an impassioned mind and heart, and feel again the power of a great biblical faith to conquer in mercy and meekness the terrors in the march of man in history.

Somehow the life and language and service of the church must embody this meaning and convey this power. Somehow in a church reborn we must find a way to celebrate this miracle of life in the life of man—to sensitize us to it, to heighten our expectations of it, to compel our participation in it—for God is very great and active in the world of man's own encounter with suffering and joy and music and tribulation.

We search for it now in a church struggling to be reborn to its task of living fully in the world—as light for the world, which is our calling by definition of Jesus himself.

There is a Catholic nun in California who struggles with the rebirth of the church, Sister Mary Corita of Los Angeles, who has published a seriograph art study of the Virgin, which she has daringly entitled, *Mary, the Juiciest Tomato of Them All.* She admits that this does make some people a little nervous, but such gaiety and daring challenge us to remove the plank from our eye, the plank that would have us take up the insipid, uninspiring work of trying to protect the reputation of Almighty God. If he is offended, he can take it. Just think what he takes of offense against his will in the freedom of man to sin, to kill, to hate, to lust. Just think what he takes of offense against his will in the freedom of the church to fight, divide, distrust itself, and sink into comfortable conformity and resist social change that would open equality to the Negro and bestow the human dignity and freedom that are the Negro's by God's having made him a man.

Still I do not think it is to spare God anything that we are bidden to righteousness. I simply do not buy the piety that says we must not sin because we hurt God. That is bad theology because it bemeans God and neglects man. It makes God a sensitive little deity who needs man as his protector. This is rubbish. Of course God is hurt by our sin, but this does not destroy him. Christ is risen. God can take our sin.

It is man who cannot take sin and is destroyed by it. Therefore, avoid evil for your sake, not God's. You and I are the ones who cannot take hatred and malice and bitterness and strife. No man can harbor these evils and nurse them without being sickened and corroded—his health and happiness destroyed. And human society cannot take injustice, callousness, and oppression without losing its security and peace. Generations of racial callousness and oppression have erupted against us in our cities. And we do not know the end of this rage. But only now do we begin to see that social health is the fruit of social responsibility, compassion, and broad justice.

Repentance of sin is an act of profoundest self-interest, for repentance is a repudiation of all the forces that destroy man and is a claim upon the power of God to defeat those forces in man and society. Confession and renunciation of sin are not for God's sake. He can take care of himself. Confession is for man's sake—for his self-respect and his self-esteem—as he reaches out for the love of God who is man's protector. That's the relationship.

Would it be altogether too secular and humanistic to say that God is for man? Somehow that does sound better than to say that God is for God, and it fits the record of God poured out for man and the world in Jesus Christ—the man for others.

In this series of radio talks and conversations with laymen we will be aiming at man and his world. That will be our focus in the weeks ahead. We will raise many questions and of course nothing we say will be final, but we will not be anxious about protecting God's sensibilities. That is not our business. Our business is to claim God's protective power and then to care in the spirit of Christ, as best we can, for the life of man in the midst of a changing world.

6.

The Trip Is Terrific, Too!

Ralph W. Wallace

At the time he delivered The Protestant Hour *sermons, Ralph W. Wallace was pastor of Macedonia Lutheran Church in Burlington, North Carolina.*

The year was 1975, the year the war in Vietnam was finally over. However, it was also the year that South Vietnam fell to the Communists.

Politics made headlines. The Watergate conspiracy ended. President Nixon exited the White House for the last time. The Watergate conspirators were given their just deserts.

President Ford survived two assassination attempts. Kidnapped heiress-turned-terrorist, Patty Hearst, was found. The Franco regime in Spain came to an end. And the United Nations issued a resolution equating Zionism with racism.

The year 1975 saw New York tumbling toward bankruptcy. Inflation was spiraling. The world was in recession.

Change was on the horizon: socially, politically, and religiously. It was a year when Americans pinned on their "win" buttons, picked up their bootstraps, and moved forward.

✦ ✦ ✦

Like the London Bridge of the first grader's game, our goal-oriented culture is falling down. Not long ago the sagging economy and the new sensitivity for humane treatment of all persons turned the glittering recruitment programs of big business on college and university campuses into riotous demonstrations. There are fewer and fewer plums to be picked by the graduates. There are fewer and fewer goals to be grabbed. Like the tower of Babel, our destination-dominated way of life is crumbling. Tomorrow is so tarnished by change and entangled in alteration that it has become a threat instead of an anticipated pleasure. Tomorrow is frustrating for those who are planning their children's education and their own retirement. Tomorrow is even more frustrating for those who are living in their tomorrows now.

A new life-style has surfaced from a slowly laid foundation and is rapidly reaching up for everyone's attention. The trip is more important than its termination. The going is more important than the goal. The driving on, the doing now, is more important than the destination. Life is seen as a series of segmented situations in which one has to move fast to make the best of them before he passes on to a new set of circumstances.

The emergence of the new life shouldn't surprise us. If our sophistication hadn't made us miss the truth of so-called platitudes, we would have realized long ago that the seeds of the new life-style were being sown by our parents, of all people. In our adolescence, when we were wrestling with academics and athletics and the acquisition of pocket money, our parents said, "These are the best years of your life. Enjoy them. Make the most of them." In our always premature parenthood, when we were worried about the proper dosage of cod liver oil and the straightness of permanent teeth and the development of proper manners, those who had reared us said, "You should enjoy them while they are young because you have them only a little while." Platitudes perhaps, but the conveyors of truth. Our elders were saying that the trip is terrific too! *The trip is terrific, too!*

The first point in our background scripture to be picked out and made clear is that *Jesus did not pray that his disciples would be delivered from a trip.* Our Lord knew that his followers would have to pack a few precious possessions and pass through this world. In fact, it was his will that the passing through be purposeful. The passing was to pervade the world with something new, with something that would change the world. He said, "I pray not that thou shouldest take them out of the world. . . . As thou hast sent me into the world, even so have I also sent them into the world."

I say this with trepidation because I too am human; I too feel insignificant, overrun, incapable of coping with the world, but it must be said. The time has been, is now, and ever shall be in which the followers of Christ should put down all their escape mechanisms and face the fact that we are travelers in this world, purposeful travelers who should replace the all-consuming alcohol and pills and lakeside retreats and hypochondria and contrived, sympathy-producing moods with a little realization of the facts. The world is here and we are in it. It is a world popping with premarital pregnancies and pre-movie speeches by the theater managers, who must threaten teenagers with police power in order to force on them the recognition of the rights of others. Our world is filled with contradictory political ideologies and opposing philosophies of action. It is a deaf world that won't listen to youth, a dumb world in which senators say, "We can't do anything." Ours is a world in which cerebral hemorrhages happen to the young and broken hips hit the elderly and pastors are kept hopping from one funeral to another because generations rise and reproduce and go. The world is here and we are to pass through it purposefully; changing this, altering that. And if we can't do anything directly we are to affect the attitudes of those on whom the world takes its toll. Christ did not pray that the disciples be delivered from a trip. He said to the Father, "I pray not that thou shouldest take them out of the world." He gives us a terrific trip, one filled with purposefulness.

"Wow, pastor, that is a tremendous theory, that is a revitalizing revelation that could make my blood run hot. But how do you put it into practice? How does one sidestep the potholes of pain and the slippery stepping stones of suffering? How does one survive the trip?" Well, whoever said that we are supposed to survive the trip? It is starting the trip and staying on the trip that is imperative, not completing it. However, there are several things that make the trip terrific too.

The second point that I want to make is that *Jesus prayed for unity in the trip.* He said, "And the glory which thou gavest me I have given them; that they may be one, even as we are one." The trip is terrific, too, because there is unity in making it. Christ was not suggesting a uniform way of life or a unireligious approach to things. He was not asking that all taste in hymnody be the same or that all doctrinal positions be cut from the same bolt or by the same pattern. He was asking that we have the same Lord and the same motivation of love to the extent that our relationships with one another are as close as his and his Father's. That would make the trip terrific!

Several Mondays ago I was tired of the trip. The post-Easter letup never had come. Illness had hit the congregation hard and had included the secretary. The treadmill was moving faster and faster and staying stationary. And to top it all off, I was to meet with the more mature ladies of the Lutheran Church Women for the purpose of presenting a program on new trends and changes in the Lutheran liturgy, a privilege that I was not sure would produce harmony. But just being there in the company of fifteen or twenty persons who represented hundreds of years of faithful service to the Lord, just being there to feel the warmth of their Christianity beneath the discussion of differences, difficulties, problems, and prospects, just being there made me resolve that I would be there again. There is a unity in the trip. Occasionally it surges under us and lifts us up and carries us on and makes us realize that *the trip is terrific, too.*

Third, Jesus prayed for *protection in the trip.* He said, "Holy Father, keep through thine own name those whom thou hast given me." The trip is terrific because there is protection in making it.

Our Lord's words bring flashbacks. There is Peter passing through perilous pits and over peaks, cooling it and copping out, declaring his faith and cutting off the ear of Caiaphas's slave and quickly going back to his nets after Easter. There is Peter confessing his faith in the bottom of a boat, betraying his Lord in a courtyard, and even playing the part of the devil with Christ. There is Peter on his way, and to him Christ said, "Simon, Simon, behold, Satan hath desired to have you, that he may sift you as wheat: But I have prayed for thee, that thy faith fail not." There is Job, one of the straightest men in Uz, one of the most prosperous men in Uz, going through his own devastating depression. His stock market crashed. His family disintegrated. His

wife turned caustic in her comments. He sat on all that
was left, a dung heap, and scraped his sores with the
husk of a plant. But at the beginning of all this God had
said to Satan, "All that he hath is in thy power; only
upon himself put not forth thine hand." There was
something about Job that God would not leave unpro-
tected, at least for a great while.

The trip may take a traumatic turn within, it may take
a tragic turn without, but we are not left comfortless. He
protects all who walk with him against Satan with all
the power represented by his holy Name. That is what
makes the trip terrific too. He protects in some way
those who are really in it.

Finally, Jesus prayed for *consecration in the trip*. He
prayed, "They are not of the world, even as I am not of
the world. Sanctify them through thy truth: thy word is
truth." The trip is terrific because there is consecration,
or sanctification, in it.

Our Lord knew that human existence contained more
perils than Pauline's. He knew that those who followed
him through human existence would be like strangers in
a small, cold town. They would feel the gaze of contented people burning on the backs of their necks with
questions like, What is he doing in my complacent corner? They would receive suspicious stares if any ripples
came to the tranquil town of contented people concur-
rent with their arrival. They would not be introduced
quickly to the healing and helpful humanness of those
who were born and bred in the ways of the town. They
would be strangers in that world as was Christ. So
Christ asked God to "hagiazein" his followers, to con-
secrate them with the truth.

That means two things. It means that God sets apart
or sanctifies his people for special tasks as he set apart

and sanctified Jeremiah as a prophet before he was born, as he set apart and sanctified the sons of Aaron as priests. God calls his followers to the vocation of being a Christian and to a million different avocations through which Christians earn their livelihood. It means that God equips or qualifies those whom he calls with the qualities of mind, heart, and character that are necessary for their vocation. In other words, as we say in the explanation of the third article of the Apostles' Creed: "I believe that I cannot by my own reason or strength believe in Jesus Christ my Lord, or come to him; but the Holy Ghost has called me through the Gospel, enlightened me by his gifts and sanctified and preserved me in true faith; in like manner as he calls, gathers, enlightens, and sanctifies the whole Christian Church on earth . . . " There is a perpetual Pentecost in the trip. That makes the trip terrific too!

You and I may want to hold on to our goals even though our goal-oriented culture is crumbling. We may desire to pursue our destination though our destination-dominated way of life is being demolished. We may still look to the termination of life for its purpose. But we shall be far happier humans if we realize that the trip is terrific too!

There is a trip. In it there is uplifting unity with others, there is protection against Satan by the Name that is the Almighty, and there is a consecration by the Spirit; not only are we called and charged but also we are clothed with that which is necessary. *The trip is terrific, too!*

7.

The Anatomy of Courage

J. Wallace Hamilton

At the time he delivered The Protestant Hour *sermons, J. Wallace Hamilton was pastor of Pasadena Community Methodist Church in St. Petersburg, Florida.*

The year was 1968. The United States intelligence ship *Pueblo* was captured by North Koreans. In Vietnam, the North Vietnamese and Vietcong launched the Tet offensive.

In sports Arthur Ashe won the U.S. Open. Catfish Hunter pitched a perfect game. And at the Summer Olympics in Mexico City, Bob Beamon set a record for the long jump, an unprecedented 29 feet 2 1/2 inches.

On July 29, 1968, Pope Paul VI issued a papal encyclical in which he banned artificial methods of birth control. Spain repealed its ancient law barring Jews. Madrid's first synagogue was dedicated. Just before Christmas, astronauts boarded the Apollo 8 spacecraft on a voyage to the moon. On Christmas Eve the astronauts read aloud, over worldwide radio, the Christmas story from the Gospel of Luke.

Martin Luther King, Jr., alluded to Moses, saying that "I might not get there with you, but we as a people will get to the promised land." The next day Dr. King was murdered by a sniper. The year 1968 will also be remembered for the assassination of presidential hopeful Robert Kennedy.

✦ ✦ ✦

Somewhere along the road where Jesus walked we come to this: "He steadfastly set his face to go to Jerusalem" (Luke 9:51).

Was Jesus afraid to go to Jerusalem? I think we have to allow that; otherwise, how can we credit him with courage? When people want to protect Christ and are reluctant to grant any shrinkage in him from the ordeal of the Cross and the events that led to it, or anything in his nature that dreaded it, recoiled from it, and wanted to escape it, they are revealing, I think, a common misunderstanding of the very qualities that make courage a virtue. Can we have courage without danger or a healthy sense of it in the one who faces it?

Rollo May the psychologist reported a survey made in the Armed Forces. It was a study undertaken to find out what made men courageous under fire. What most of the G.I.'s already knew and what the psychologists found out was that the most courageous men on the battlefield were not those who had no fear; on the contrary, they were the men who were most able and honest to acknowledge how scared they really were. A good example is the soldier who told his shaking knees that if they just knew where he were going to take them, they would shake sure enough. Someone wrote a little verse about that:

> It's not exactly courage
> If you're not a bit afraid
> To climb the towering mountain
> Or descend into the glade.
> But this is really courage,
> At least I call it so,
> To say, "I fear that mountain,
> But just the same, I'll go."

I.

Today we are to think about the anatomy of courage. Jesus set his face to go to Jerusalem. He knew the danger there, had a healthy man's fear of it, but steadfastly he set his face to go. Now courage is one virtue universally accepted and admired. I suppose there has never been a nation or an age in which courage was not exalted. The Indians called their young men "braves." The Spartans measured their manhood by it, and in Latin the word for valor is "virtus," the root word from which we get "virtue." Valor and virtue were the same thing. And we must remember that while there are many kinds of courage, there is in all of them some element of virtue.

I suppose our ideas of courage change somewhat as we grow older. When we are very young our instinctive admiration goes out to those who brave physical dangers. We never get over that—the exciting adventures of men risking their lives in all kinds of daring enterprises, *the courage of competition.* Bull fighters have it, mountain climbers, trapeze artists, maniacs of the speedways on land and water, test pilots, astronauts. What courage it takes in a man to climb into a capsule to be blasted a hundred and fifty miles above the earth where a small mechanical failure can trigger instant death or leave him going around and around the earth forever. Physical courage is exciting, often dramatic. And our hunger for heroes in that area will never diminish.

II.

It's only a step from the courage of competition to *the courage of conflict.* In a world so full of war as ours is, the bravery of the battlefield has been highly and universally exalted. What magnificent bravery the centuries have seen! We remember Garibaldi and his appeal to the sons of Italy. He offered nothing, he said, but "hunger, thirst, forced marches, battles and death." And they went. Or Winston Churchill in England's darkest hour: "We shall defend our island. . . . We shall never surrender." And they didn't. Hitler had the hammer, but Britain had the heart, and by the sheer bulldog courage of common people it turned the darkest hour into the finest. We remember the battle cry of Verdun, "They shall not pass." More than half a million Frenchmen fell there, and even as they fell they shouted, "They shall not pass." And they didn't. As far back in history as you want to go men have turned their faces toward some kind of Jerusalem, knowing beforehand that they would die there, but they went. The courage of conflict is not over. It remains an undiminished force and is expressed in many forms.

Four chaplains on the troopship *Dorchester* torpedoed in the nighttime off the coast of Greenland—two Protestant, one Catholic priest, and a Jewish rabbi— helped to man the lifeboats, gave up their own lifejackets when the supply was gone, and were last seen by the survivors standing on the slanting deck, arms linked together singing hymns, saying prayers as the ship went down and disappeared in the sea. Four men, different faiths, yet in the crisis—one. There was nothing in the regulation book requiring chaplains to give up their lifejackets. But there was another Book in which they all believed. No, the courage of conflict is not diminished. Every day out of Vietnam come stories of magnificent gallantry.

There was a funeral up in Arlington, a young Army sergeant, the father of three children, posthumously awarded the Medal of Honor. . . . On a rice paddy in Vietnam he had thrown himself on a live mine, absorbed the full blast of it, and saved the lives of his comrades. When our President gave the medal to the young widow holding back her tears, he said, "You're a brave young woman." She said, "Mr. President, I have to be brave because he was brave." And in that poignant little speech is listed another kind of courage not too often recognized, a young woman going home with three children to be mother and father to. Call it *the courage of the commonplace,* often demanding a greater gallantry on a thousand unseen battlefields where no drums beat and no awards are given; the courage of the commonplace—loneliness, sickness, bereavement.

How brave some people are. Life sometimes drafts us to bear an unexpected load, to carry another person's cross, and to share the steadfastness of ordinary people in monotonous situations. Such bravery gives you a feeling of exhilaration, makes you proud to belong to such a breed who for all our pettiness and failures have still within us the capacity for something God-like and divine.

III.

Move up another step, to *the courage of conscience,* to heroes of history who for conscience' sake set their faces toward some Jerusalem. The signers of the Declaration of Independence were brave men, as brave as anyone on any battlefield. They knew the document they were signing was pure treason, punishable by death. They had no assurance that they would be supported by their countrymen, but they went right down the line. They walked boldly to the table and put down their lives with their names, for conscience' sake, with conviction.

The history of the church is not without its pages of valor and virtue. Often we need to remind ourselves that our faith now lives with some measure of strength only because some brave men were willing to put down their lives for it. The church began in the flames of martyrdom. Only one of the original Disciples died a natural death. Forty percent of the New Testament was written in prison.

One of the popes in Rome said to a visiting dignitary who had come to the Vatican to purchase some relics for his chapel, "You want some Christian relics? Go then to the Colosseum, gather up some dust. It's all martyred dust," the dust of men and women who gave their lives for their faith. And there has been a long line of martyrs since.

You sometimes wonder if we're losing this out of our lives, the courage of Christian conscience. Dean Inge said, "We're losing our Christianity because Christianity is a religion for heroes, and we are just good-natured people who want to be left alone and have a good time." Is that true? I don't know. I know the church has been very timid in spots, but I also know there are still brave voices in the church, in pulpit and in pew, people who are ready to put down their lives for Christ and for his cause.

Take a moment to look at *the courage of the cross*. Isn't it odd, almost ironic, that we are so much accustomed to thinking of Christ as presenting the tender graces, the gentle aspects of life, that we overlook the majestic strength in him, the vigor, the restrained power, which was the first and foremost effect he had on friend and foe alike? If Jesus were like what some artists have pictured him, however did he manage to get himself crucified? All that men call heroic was in him, physical courage. He set his face toward Jerusalem knowing what would happen there. He had seen many crosses and victims die on them, some of his own countrymen. He had seen the Romans push his people around, and often his blood burned hot in him at the indignities heaped on them. The cross was a Roman instrument of torture; a nail was driven into a man's hand to hang from until he died. "If it be possible, let the cup pass." But he went. "If I be lifted up, I will draw men." Has he?

In the play "Will Shakespeare," Queen Elizabeth is made to say, "I'll not bow to the gentle Jesus of the women, I. But to the man who hung twixt earth and heaven six mortal hours yet ruled his soul and body so that when the sponge blessed his cracked lips with promise of relief He would not drink. He turned his head away and would not drink, spat out the anodyne and would not drink. This was God for kings and queens, and Him I follow." "Behold the man," said Pilate. He knew bravery when he saw it, even if he didn't have it.

This was moral courage too, the courage of conscience and conviction. He could have died in his bed. He could have hied himself off to the mountains, taught his disciples under a tree as Buddha did. He was no ascetic running away from life. And when he went to Jerusalem he meant business there. He knew the evil that gripped his countrymen was concentrated and centered in a ruling clique in that city, and to the dismay of his disciples he came to grips with it, smoked it out, made it smite him. And there he hangs taut against the wood, the just for the unjust that he might bring us to God.

There is more than courage in the cross, of course; there is a profound depth in it, an inexhaustible manysidedness. But nothing in the world has nerved men so much, made them so strong to face the battle, as this deed upon a hill. When someone goes out to suffer and die for us it touches the deepest feeling in us. And it takes a very hard heart to be unmoved by it.

An archbishop of Paris stood in the pulpit of Notre Dame Cathedral. He was there to preach the sermon, and his whole sermon was built around a story. Thirty years before, he said, three young tourists had come into this cathedral. They were rough, rude, cynical men who thought all religion was a racket. Two of them dared a third to go into the confession box and make a bogus confession to the priest. They dared him to do it, bet him that he didn't have the nerve. But to win the bet, he did. He tried to fool the old priest, but the priest knew that what he was saying was a lie. He listened to the false confession, sensed the arrogance in the man's attitude, and said, "Very well, my son. Every confession requires a penance, and this will be yours. I ask you to go into the chapel, stand before the Crucifix, look into the face of the crucified Christ and say, 'all this you did for me, and I don't care a damn.'"

The young man swaggered out of the confessional to his friends to claim the bet, but they insisted that before they paid him he would have to finish the performance, complete the penance. He went into the chapel, looked into the face of Christ, and began, "All this you did for me, and I . . . " He couldn't say it. He never finished the sentence. It began for him a painful experience that changed his life and finally brought him into the priesthood. And the archbishop telling the story leaned over the pulpit and said, "That young man was this man who

65

stands before you to preach." "If I be lifted up, I will draw men." Has he? Has he won your heart, claimed your life? It takes a hard heart to be unmoved by this.

> God of grace and God of glory,
> On Thy people pour Thy power;
> Crown Thine ancient Church's story;
> Bring its bud to glorious flower.
> Grant us wisdom, grant us courage,
> For the facing of this hour. Amen.

8.

The Church: The Glorious Liberty of the Children of God

Patricia McClurg

At the time she delivered The Protestant Hour *sermons, Patricia McClurg was administrative director of the Presbyterian General Assembly Mission Board.*

The year was 1978, a year of political revolt and human rights. Demonstrations and riots swept Iran as Muslim fundamentalists called for the overthrow of the Shah. Hard-line Communists seized power in Afghanistan, and United States planes dropped French and Belgian paratroopers in Zaire.

This was the year of three popes. Pope Paul VI died on August 6. Pope John Paul I was elected on August 26, only to reign one month before he died. On October 23, Pope John Paul II was elected.

Israeli prime minister Menachem Begin and Egyptian president Anwar Sadat met with President Jimmy Carter at Camp David to work out a plan for peace in the Middle East.

The Supreme Court ruled that college admission policies that favor minorities were constitutional. The Church of Jesus Christ of Latter Day Saints ordained black priests for the first time. The push was on to ratify the Equal Rights Amendment. One hundred thousand marched on Washington in support.

✦ ✦ ✦

A church *is* family and the members are *one* in Jesus Christ and *one* in that all members of this family have been *liberated* to care about one another.

Jesus began his prophetic ministry in the synagogue at Nazareth by reading the opening lines of this passage from the prophet Isaiah:

> The Spirit of the Lord God is upon me,
>   because the Lord has anointed me
> to bring good tidings to the afflicted;
>   he has sent me to bind up the brokenhearted,
> to proclaim liberty to the captives,
>   and the opening of the prison to those
>   who are bound;
> To proclaim the year of the Lord's favor
>   and the day of vengeance of our God;
>   to comfort all who mourn;
> to grant to those who mourn in Zion—
>   to give them a garland instead of ashes,
> the oil of gladness instead of mourning,
>   the mantle of praise instead of a faint spirit;
> that they may be called oaks of righteousness,
>   the planting of the Lord, that he may be glorified.
>
> (Isa. 61:1-3)

Jesus used this passage to outline his own mission in the world, stating, "Today this scripture has been fulfilled in your hearing." And later in his ministry he called the church, the family of God, to proclaim by word and deed that Christ gave himself to set people free from sin and self-hatred, from ignorance and disease, from all forms of oppression, and even from death.

The intensely personal tone of this passage from Isaiah does not constitute a summons, a *demand;* it is rather a proclamation, an announcement, that the very kingdom of God is pressing in on the events and affairs of this world.

Liberation. Good tidings to the afflicted and the poor. Liberty to the captives, to those who are oppressed. Healing for the brokenhearted. Comfort for those who mourn.

This scripture was read by Jesus in the segregated synagogue in Nazareth—a place that put a dividing wall between Jew and Gentile, man and woman, priest and layperson. Jesus came to change that. In fact, with his inaugural sermon he pronounced that the change had already taken place. With his being and his life he planted the revolutionary seed which continues to germinate today in behalf of the liberation of all people from the dehumanizing compartments we tend to put folks into; the liberation of all people to be children of God, brothers and sisters of one another, the glorious liberty of the children of God. Jesus came to change things, and the impact, the reverberations, of his ministry among us go on still. Jesus, the servant as Isaiah had portrayed him, was sent primarily for the sake of the oppressed and the downhearted.

He spoke a word to those who were enslaved and he spoke a word to those who were discontent with the way things were; and he lived a life in behalf of those who were depressed and brokenhearted. Good news. Release to the captives. You are free at last, free at last.

There were those in Israel who grieved over the wretchedness of Israel's fate in world history. There were those in Israel who were discontent with the nation's meager achievement in behalf of justice. Jesus came to speak and live a word and way of hope and comfort for those who would mourn like that over the fate of God's family.

The prophet Isaiah dreamed of the day when the lion and the lamb would lie down together, when the tendency of the strong to devour the weak would be destroyed; and Jesus announced, This is the dawning of that day of the glorious liberty of the children of God, free from the sin of division and oppression, free for caring about and loving God and one another.

That liberation event is not yet complete, but it has begun and it cannot be stopped. To be a part of the family of the people of God is to be a part of that ever-moving-onward freedom march. And the intent, the faith intent, *is* that all will be free to be and to become, bound together in a single reality called the people of God, committed together to give ourselves in relationship to one another, where the strong will not devour the weak, but will enable the weak to be strong also.

Free *from* the powers that deform and destroy human life. Free from divisiveness and bitterness. Free *for* caring about and building up one another.

The seed has been planted. As Isaiah spoke that phrase, we are "the planting of the Lord." The church is the band of those who are ever moving toward harvest time.

Today I want to pick up on a couple of threads that are a part of that family tapestry of deliverance, to depict just a little of what it means to be on this freedom march. I have selected a couple of threads that happen to be woven into our own nation's history—slavery and the role of women.

It may be helpful to remember that the decisive moment in Israel's history was God's act of divine redemption, which brought forth a band of slaves from Egypt. Slavery was economically and socially an integral part of the ancient Near Eastern world, and the Hebrews had some firsthand experience with how that felt. Slaves were a commodity, to be bought, sold, and branded like cattle. Children were sold. People sold themselves or worked their way into slavery by being captives of a war or captives of interest rates more outrageous than even we today know—interest rates of 20 to 35 percent. As *Amos* spoke of it, "They sell the righteous for silver, and the needy for a pair of shoes."

Because of their experience as slaves and because of the will of their Lord, the Hebrews' laws on slavery, as those are recorded in the Old Testament, are significantly different from those of neighboring peoples in that day. Israel could not quite disregard the fact that a slave was a human being. Many of the Hebrew slavery laws show a remarkable concern for the rights, limited though they may be, of the dispossessed, those who are bought and sold. The period of forced slavery of the defaulting debtor was limited to six years. There was the law of the Year of Jubilee, unparalleled in the ancient Near East, the year when all citizens had the opportunity of freedom, when each slave could return to his or her family.

Their experience of slavery and the will of their Lord made an impact on the laws of Israel. Their laws were more humane. But it was slavery nonetheless, and slavery disrupted the community, the household of God.

Jesus read the scripture—release to the captives—and set in motion a revolution, the waves of which have lapped up to the shores of our own nation. And that battle is now in the hands of the people of God, who are to be brothers and sisters, not slaves and masters.

Presidents in our nation have made proclamations and even gone to war; preachers have marched; brave people have run underground railroads and have refused to stay in a place called "the back of the bus"; for more than two centuries a host of brothers and sisters have made sacrifices so that the rest of us can join black and white and brown and yellow and red hands. And as we in this land join the march for the oppressed, to enable the good tidings of Jesus to make an impact in our towns and cities, we join also the worldwide family of those who struggle for rights for all persons in Korea, South Africa, Russia, Brazil, or wherever. The people of God are not to be slaves or masters. They are to be brothers and sisters.

And we have some special concern in behalf of the sisters of this world. Today in this land and in the church there are disagreements among us about how the sister, the woman, should fit in behalf of the health and wholeness of the covenant community, the family of the people of God.

Both slaves and women were *stirred* in the first century by aspirations of emancipation. A phrase of the Hebrew in this Isaiah passage read by Jesus can be translated quite literally "the opening of the eyes to them that are bound." The eyes of these slaves and these women were opened and they saw their own bondage. They saw also the promised land. The light of that vision of the family of God cannot be put out.

For women, a whole lot of the yearning for freedom revolves around their own nuclear family relationships. That's been the case for a long time. The Israelite family was held together by the central and dominant father figure, who even possessed the right, under certain conditions, to destroy members of his family, to offer his son as a sacrifice; it was the father, the husband, who alone had the right of divorce. Sons were much more valued than were daughters, and the right of inheritance belonged to the male members of the family. Women were not qualified to testify as witnesses and were barred from serving in any official capacity at the temple. Not only were women's rights limited by law and in practice; certain characteristics were assigned to women to help re-enforce that legislated subservient role—a woman was to be discreet, gracious, and loyal (as well as beautiful, of course). Negatively women were pictured as being noisy, the cause of sin, contentious, gossipy. As those stereotypes continue to come at us on the T.V. screen, in jokes, and in the midst of daily assumptions about life together, today it would not seem to be the case that women have come a long way. In this land of ours, the *vote* was won, but as astounding as it may seem, there is trouble now about an amendment that asks simply for equal rights for women.

I believe that it is fair to say that the writers of the New Testament tended to accept the Old Testament view of women's subordination to men. Paul didn't want some women speaking in church. Women generally were to be treated as mothers and sisters had always been treated.

But the seed of revolution was planted. Although it ran counter to the customs of his time, it is clear that Jesus took women seriously as persons, as human beings, and spent a large part of his ministry among them; his ministry, which was good tidings to the afflicted, liberty for those who are oppressed.

The gospel was available—for rich and poor, female and male, slave and free—for there was a new family

73

abornin', coming into being, God's own kingdom pressing on in the events and affairs of this world.

God liberates us from sin, that being out of harmony
with him and out of harmony with us. And God liberates us from the consequences of sin—the oppressing,
the grinding down, the limiting, the stunting of the
growth of anyone who is human. God calls us into a
new family, where there is abundant life, where there
are whole, healthy people, women and men, living up to
their full potential.

The early church grew even among, and especially
among, those of the lower class of society—those who
were called slave and those who were called women.
And the reverberations of that revolution, that planting
of the Lord, go on yet today. Something happens in that
new family life in Christ that abolishes differences that
divide us and thwart our development as human beings.
Something happens in that new family "in the Lord"
that makes us all mutually interdependent with one
another and with him. To be a part of this family called
the people of God is to be a part of beating down, over-
coming, the limitations that sin and culture have placed
upon us.

Liberty—not to be confined or oppressed. Good tidings, Good News—of what God has done, is doing, and
will surely accomplish. We await and press on toward
the grand finale in confident hope. The new family. The
new age working itself out in these states of ours and
around the planet Earth.

That day long ago in Nazareth Jesus brought encour-
agement, a view of the future that has given centuries of
people the endurance and the hardheaded hope that will
see us through to the fulfillment of Isaiah's dream of the
day when the lion and the lamb will lie down together,

when the sinful inclination of the strong to devour the weak will be no more.

This is no free-falling, no free-floating liberation—there is nothing libertine about it. It is a binding liberation, issuing in a new family which requires mutual commitment, the recognition of mutual dependence, of a shared suffering and of the power of love to knit together all parts of the body. A community intimately bound together in which there is neither Jew nor Gentile, slave nor master, male nor female. A community of righteousness which reaches out to help and incorporate those who have had their rights taken away from them. Freedom from fear, freedom from that which deforms human life, from that which inhibits; and freedom for that which binds us together as sisters and brothers.

Jesus went to Nazareth where he had been brought up and he went to the synagogue on the Sabbath day as was his habit. When he stood up to read the lesson of the day, he was handed the scroll of the prophet Isaiah. Good news—healing and comfort of the downhearted, liberty to the captives. Then he said, Today this text has come true. People are not to be put into restrictive boxes anymore. The glorious liberty of the children of God—brothers and sisters, by the planning of the Lord—will be accomplished.

9.

What Shall I Do with Him?

Samuel M. Shoemaker

At the time he delivered The Protestant Hour *sermons, Samuel M. Shoemaker was rector of Calvary Episcopal Church in Pittsburgh, Pennsylvania.*

The year was 1960 . . . the Cold War had taken a turn. Americans focused on Cuba and its new leader, Fidel Castro, who, it was feared, had Communist ties.

Soviet leader Khrushchev in an address to the U.N. spoke of the possibility of nuclear war. Schoolchildren were drilled in duck-and-cover procedures in the event of a nuclear attack.

Race relations were heating up. Sit-ins at segregated restaurants were a common occurrence in the South. On March 1, 1960, one thousand blacks assembled at the Confederate capital in Montgomery, Alabama, to pray and sing "The Star Spangled Banner."

In 1960, movie audiences were drawn to two films set in ancient Rome—the Oscar winning *Ben Hur* and Stanley Kubrick's *Spartacus*. These movies asked the viewer to consider what we are to make of this man called King of the Jews. What verdict will be rendered?

Pilate saith unto them, What shall I do then with Jesus which is called Christ? (Matt. 27:22)

We remember today what is called the "triumphal entry" of Jesus into Jerusalem. He and his little company of loyal followers had made their way down from Galilee to Judea. Today they come up over the brow of the hills to the east of the city, and enter it. His fame has preceded him, and the crowds are out to see the excitement. They cut branches off the trees to throw in his path.

Jesus seems to have had a deep-seated conviction that he believed was from God that he should go right into the great city of Jerusalem and ask for a verdict. All around him are disturbed and troubled minds. His own company will huddle together for warmth and safety at one time, flee out of fear at another, standing dazed and helpless as the drama unfolds and comes to the climax of the cross, dispersing after this great calamity, and coming together again only after the Resurrection. There are the chief priests and elders of the people of the Jewish church-state, who oppose Jesus with a show of loyalty to Rome, but really because his spiritual power has stung their consciences and enraged them against him. There is Pilate, with all the paraphernalia of Rome behind him, and its domination of a little, subject nation.

Pilate pretends justice, for he is frightened by the dream and warning of his wife; but he fears to stand against the public clamor for Jesus' crucifixion. The crowd does not know what to think or believe. They have heard of his power: But the religious and political authorities both seem to be against him. Turmoil is in every mind and on every face. Only one Face is calm and strong and without fear. He knows he is doing exactly what he ought to be doing, what the Father wants him to do. He moves through the crowds who are friendly, through the opposers who cry for his blood, with a majesty and quietness all his own. He has no worldly power to support him, nothing but God and sheer spiritual power. The whole story seems to be about their judgment of him. The priests, Pilate, and the people, all think so. We know now that the story is really about his judgment of them.

"What shall I do then with Jesus which is called Christ?" That is what Pilate asked. How little did Pilate know he was posing the greatest question that can ever be posed to an individual or a nation. Outwardly, of course, Pilate had, as he said, "power to crucify thee, and . . . power to release thee." What would happen to Jesus' human life and physical body was completely at the mercy of the Roman governor. But even then one feels that Pilate knew he stood in the presence of the kind of goodness and spiritual power over which he had no control whatever. His question sounds as if it contained nothing but the ruthless power of Rome, waiting to decide the fate of a spiritual nonconformer from up country. His wife's warnings disturbed Pilate; for like many irreligious men, he was superstitious, and afraid of her dream. There was, I think, a kind of trembling note in his question, "What shall I do then with Jesus which is called Christ?" He had Jesus on his hands. It was difficult enough to make a legal decision about him, but Pilate knew the real decision was a moral one. I wonder whether Pilate may have had some premonition that history would turn the tables, and he—Pilate— would go down to infamy forever, the tables completely turned, and his name imbedded in the very creed of Christendom, "Crucified under Pontius Pilate."

It was not only the priests and Pilate and the people of that day who had Jesus on their hands—you and I have Jesus on our hands, and we must ask and we must answer that very same question: What shall I do then with Jesus which is called Christ? For during twenty centuries he has been the inspiration for almost every reform that has been for the benefit of mankind. He has changed and reclaimed almost every kind of human weakness and sinfulness. He is the very symbol of the best that we know. Someone has said that "he has become entangled in our instincts." Western civilization, with its amazing freedom, owes the very best things in its life directly to him. So it is not into the ancient city of Jerusalem that he rides today, asking for a verdict: It is into your heart and mine. He did not alone incarnate an issue for men long ago; he incarnates it today. Today, as then, it is not he who is on trial but ourselves. You may know the story of the man who visited the Salon Carre, the room in the Louvre in Paris where hang some of the masterpieces of the world. He looked at them superciliously and said to a guard, "I don't think they are so wonderful." And the guard replied, "They are not on trial: you are."

What shall I do then about Jesus Christ?

First, I must accept him on his own conditions and his own terms. Kierkegaard was right when he said there were only two possible attitudes toward him: to believe in him and accept him, or else to be "offended" in him. To offer him the kind of lip service and routine discipleship that some people offer him, who call themselves Christians, is as an insult to him. He came from high heaven; he lived his life; he died on Calvary, for you and for me. Do you think casualness about his worship and his work in the world, going to church when I "feel" like it and giving whatever I do not think I need for myself, is any response to what he did for me?

Moreover we cannot take him as just another good teacher whose way of life is beautiful and whose compassion toward the poor and downtrodden leads me to follow him in lowly service—certainly this, but ever so much more. For it was his faith that he was the divine Son of God.

When his own followers called him Son of God, he told them they were guided by the Holy Spirit in what they had said. Concerning his cross, he said he had come as a "ransom for many" and was pouring out his blood "for many for the remission of sins." Here is no mere good example: Here is an atoning Savior, who three days after his crucifixion was raised from the dead. What we shall do with him depends finally on who we think he is. He makes the terms on which we serve him. We must begin by living up to all the meanings we see in him. If, as yet, we cannot accept him as divine Lord and Savior, let us begin where we can. The approach to this is not, I think, an authoritarian approach, but an experimental one. We begin by giving as much of ourselves as we can to as much of Jesus Christ as we understand. This is honest; it is experimental; it leaves room for growth.

Second, we must accept him by the commitment of ourselves to him and to his will. We shall find we cannot accept mere intellectual statements about him unless we turn these at once into personal commitment to him. Theological conclusions have immediate moral and personal consequences. If Jesus is who he says he is, nothing will do but the unconditional surrender of myself to him and to his will so far as I can understand it—and the willingness to do it is the first condition of understanding it: "If any man will do his will, he shall know of the doctrine" (John 7:17).

Let us look honestly at our lives in the light of his demand for humility, for love, for sacrifice, for truthfulness, for unselfishness, for forgiveness. We content ourselves—something we often do by comparing ourselves with other people, only to conclude that we are doing as well as "the next one." But suppose the "next one" were Jesus himself. Too many of us who call ourselves Christians are only doing enough to "get by." We do not want to be counted pagans, so we keep a church connection. But our hearts are far from it. Add up what you spend for the care of the hair on your head during a year, and compare it with what you give to carry the Christian message overseas. We know we should do better. Someday we mean to.

We live our lives in the light of that faint hope, that unfulfilled promise. We have heard his voice calling to us, one time when we walked alone in the country, or through the words of Scripture, or through the lips of someone speaking in his Name. We heard it above the din of other human voices on all sides of us. But unless it is heeded, it begins to grow dim. Our postponed discipleship, our delayed commitment, our meaning to do something about it some day, are just not good enough. We know there is a kind of unbreakable affinity between him and us; we know what we should do. Fear, conventionality, caution, the siren voices of this world have kept us from it. He calls to you and to me today to surrender our lives to him in faith, to mend our ways, to begin a true discipleship as a Christian.

Every one that I know whose discipleship has resulted in real power and service has somewhere had to pass through what for that person corresponded to the cross—some crisis of self-denial and self-giving. Jesus is asking for a verdict from you now, today. You can kneel by your desk or your bed, you can draw your car to a stop by the roadside, you can go into a church and kneel before God's altar—the circumstance matters not at all. What matters is the depth of surrender with which you give over your heart, your life, your very innermost soul, and your future to him in one full act of self-surrender.

Third, we must accept him by sharing in the task he set for his people in the world. He wanted every last man, woman, and child in the world to know him, to love and serve him, and to love and serve one another. He wanted to see the world a place where justice, brotherhood, right relations, goodness, and peace would prevail. He knew this could not come about by any fiat, and that it would often be hindered by the routines and conservatism of the church itself. He gave the people about him a completely fresh grasp upon God and his goodness. He cut through all the minutiae of legalism into which religion about him had sunk and said, "Love God with all your hearts—and your neighbor as yourself." He set about changing individuals and immediate human relations. He knew that, in the end, converted people in touch with him would do away with slavery and oppression and social evil, which grows up among aggregates of people.

Do you hold back on him in this? Is he way out beyond where you are willing to go? There is a fake and counterfeit pattern of reform in the world. It is called communism. One of the things it trades on is our failures and follies in the West. No man can anywhere oppress or try to hold down individuals or races without contributing to communism's success in the world. If you will not take Christ's way voluntarily, you may have to take communism's way involuntarily—some evils can and must be remedied now.

God calls us by love if we will heed him. He calls us by judgment, which is a sterner form of love, if we do not heed him. We are on trial before Christ and before the bar of the world; we who call ourselves Christians, and are content to live along with old evils that should long ago have been banished. If our nation were overtly at war, we should change all our personal habits and sacrifice to win the war. We are in a far greater war than that, really. It is the war between Light and Darkness; between freedom and oppression; between decent treatment for little children, underprivileged people, and dumb animals, all around the world, as against cruelty and indifference; between selfish indulgence of our bodies with needless luxuries and care for people who starve. If these folk were on our doorsteps we would probably do something. They are on our doorsteps. If we wanted to banish the sickness, poverty, and fear that grips vast portions of the world, especially in Southern Asia and Africa, we could. The means are here if the caring were here. We won't do it unless, or until, Christ is allowed to touch our hearts—the hundreds of us, thousands of us, who have been daring to call ourselves Christians.

Today Christ is asking us when we are going to begin to live like Christians. Get into the church, and help wake it up. So much of the church is more like the world than it is like the Kingdom. Yet we need the multiplied force of millions of us working together to do this vast thing, which needs to be done, for the bodies and for the minds and for the souls of men all over the face of the earth.

Whether we shall measure up to beginning this, and whether we shall have the staying power to keep on with it, goes back to our personal answer to that question, What shall I do then with Jesus which is called Christ? Everything that really matters in the world is summed up in him. If we decided aright what to do about him, everything else would begin to come right. There would still be trial and trouble, but there would not be defeat and disaster. It all begins in an intensely personal commitment to Jesus Christ. But it does not end there. He made it very clear that the way we treat our fellowmen is the real measure of our commitment to him. A merely private faith for our own comfort will more likely damn us than save us. The anguish of our world cannot be imagined, the fear, the cruelty, the wickedness, the personal indifference to the fate of others.

Where are the Christians? Where is the church? Just where you and I are. Not to the gates of Jerusalem alone does Jesus ride today, but to the gates of our hearts. There he waits, knocking, knocking. His knuckles must be raw by now. The gentle rap has been so long smothered by contemporary rivals that some of us can hardly hear it. But he goes on standing there. He is asking for a verdict from you—for him, or against him. He is waiting for an answer from you. Today.

10.

Do Not Cling to Me

Edmund Steimle

At the time he delivered The Protestant Hour *sermons, Edmund Steimle was the Brown Professor of Homiletics at Union Theological Seminary in New York.*

On Easter Sunday 1973, Americans prayed in thanks. United States involvement in the Vietnam War had ended. The first planeload of American POW's had returned home. Many of the young men and women from the military had come back safely to United States soil.

In January 1973 Richard Nixon was sworn in for his second term. In his inaugural speech he told us to ask, "not just how can government help, but how can I help." Several months after his inauguration, the Watergate affair exploded.

The past was on the minds of Americans. Moviegoers enjoyed *American Graffiti* and *The Sting.* On television "All in the Family" opened with Archie and Edith singing "Those Were the Days."

Americans were interested in the simple life. The yearning for the simplicity of the past extended into religious life. Televangelism was peaking. Jim Bakker railed against "modernist preachers," and Jerry Falwell treated us to "The Old Time Gospel Hour." Membership in mainline churches and enrollment in seminaries was in decline. Why? Do we know?

In 1973 there was an overwhelming allure to return to the past, to the appeal of a simple gospel, one that would take the Bible simply and literally. But the Easter story in John presents a different picture.

As I was mulling over this sermon on the meeting between Mary Magdalene and the risen Lord outside the empty tomb, I happened to be flying from Chicago to New York on a fantastically brilliant, clear night. Even at 33,000 feet, the thousands of sparkling lights on the ground below seemed so close you could almost sense the people living in and around them: people watching T.V. in the early evening, friends visiting, children doing homework, men at their basement work-benches, cars darting here and there. And I thought suddenly, how utterly absurd to imagine that any of them could care one bit about the scene outside an empty tomb, or about what Mary said to Jesus or what Jesus said in reply, as compared with their interesting "All in the Family," the rising cost of food in the supermarket, the latest bit of town gossip, or the fortunes of the local high school basketball team.

And yet virtually all of them would be concerned about the tension between the old and the new, the good old days and the perplexing present, the tension between old life-styles and new ones, between old moral standards and new ones, between a fairly stable and simple past and an almost terrifying present with its rapidly changing customs, morals, standards.

And most of them over thirty, anyway, would want to cling to the old and resist the everchanging new. At least so it seems if the temper of today is accurately reflected in the popularity of nostalgic musicals like "No, No, Nanette," and "Oh Coward," or in the spate of recordings of songs of the 30s, 40s, 50s, or in the rising popularity of conservative religious groups, or in the yen for gospel songs like "Amazing Grace," which reflect an older, simpler kind of religion. When radical change comes along and hits us almost every day, it's understandable that we seek reassurance and stability by clinging to the past. And that does bring us directly to the story of Mary Magdalene and Jesus outside an empty tomb on Easter morning.

It was dark there when Mary first came to the tomb to grieve and mourn a lost friend. But darkness was no new experience for Mary. Much of her life she had spent as a prostitute—or so most students of the New Testament seem to agree. And even if she wasn't, she had, apparently, been possessed by demons—distraught, emotionally unstable, perhaps. And although her friend, Jesus, had driven out the demons, who knows whether they had returned or not. At least the only light in the darkness of her life had come at the hands of him who was now dead. No question about that. Dead. She had felt each nail in his flesh as if it had been driven into her own. The darkness which covered the earth at the time of his death had not turned to light for Mary. It was dark there beside the tomb.

But not so dark that she could not see that the stone had been rolled away from the entrance. This did not cheer her. It was startling. Queer. Someone must have come and opened the tomb and taken off with the body. So she ran back to the friends of her friend, Peter and John, and told them the strange news. They ran to the tomb and saw the queer scene for themselves—and went away. And Mary was left weeping by an empty tomb alone.

Easter is not the celebration of an empty tomb. There is no comfort, no reassurance in an empty tomb. If that's all there is to the Easter story we are left weeping along with Mary.

But as she wept, she felt the presence of someone else, some figure standing beside her, saying in a voice she did not recognize, "Why are you weeping?" Thinking it might be the voice of a gardener, she replied, "Sir, if you have carried him off, tell me where you have laid him and I will take him away."

Then came the moment when the darkness was split in two, when sun and moon and stars all shone together, when the heavens were filled with the sound of bells, and angel choirs sang their hallelujahs . . . when the voice of the gardener became the voice of Jesus as he simply called her by name, "Mary." Now the past was alive again. The brightness he had brought into the darkness of her life was flooding the world again. Death—strangely, miraculously—had not taken his life and love from her after all. He was *there*—calling her by name!

And this is what Easter is all about, isn't it? Not just an empty tomb, but a presence, a person, a voice calling each of us by name. Not just a fact, a rather sterile fact, actually, that Christ is risen from the dead, but that Christ is alive to call you by name, to call me by name, for all our names are caught up in that one name, "Mary."

And this is why the celebrations, why the Easter Eucharist with Christ saying to each one of us individually, "given for you . . . shed for you"; this is why the hallelujahs and the choirs and the altars banked with flowers. A voice out of death calling you by name in reassurance and hope. That despite all that seems to deny it, he who went about teaching and healing, he who went about telling those strange and disturbing parables, he who faced trial, suffering, and death—this same Jesus is alive today calling you by name: "Mary." And light and life and joy and hope break the darkness into bits.

But then . . . we're not sure quite what happened. Maybe Mary reached out her hand to touch him, or maybe she started to throw her arms around his feet—whatever it was, Jesus replied suddenly, "Don't cling to me."

The rebuke sounds strange at first. No doubt Mary simply wanted to be sure that it was the same Jesus she had known before he died. And that's understandable. Indeed a number of details in the Resurrection stories make that precise point: Jesus' eating with them, Thomas wanting to put his hand into Jesus' side—in order to be sure that this was not some apparition or vision but a new reality by which this same Jesus of Nazareth whom they had seen die was now alive among them.

But Mary was not to cling to the Jesus of the past. It was the same Jesus who had brought light into the darkness of her life. But now something new had entered the picture. Things had changed radically. Mary was now living in a new and bewildering age. Nothing could ever be the same again, never again as it had been before he died. Now he tells her, "I am ascending to my Father and your Father, to my God and your God." And Mary could hardly be expected to understand what all that meant, except that it must be a strange new world where he would be separated from her, at least as she had always known him, but that he would be present for her in new and strange and unpredictable ways. A new thing was emerging out of the old and familiar ways of the past and she would have to adjust to that. It must have been scary.

And one can understand Mary, I suspect. Our feelings about the amazing wonder of God calling each of us by name—this is what Easter is all about. And we'd simply like to cling to that. Cling to the reassurance and the hope. Cling to the hallelujahs and the music and the flowers, and let that be the end of it. Like Peter, who, enraptured by the vision on the Mount of Transfiguration, wanted to settle down and spend his days worshiping there forever. But there was misery on the plain below. Tough and unpredictable problems. And Jesus led him down from the mountain to the misery on the plain below. "Don't cling to me."

So later on that first Easter day, Jesus appeared to the disciples and said, "Peace be unto you: as my Father hath sent me, even so send I you." There was to be no basking in the light of a resurrected Lord. No clinging to the joy of his presence. But a bombshell instead: "As my Father hath sent me, even so send I you." And that meant out into the unpredictable misery of life—and possibly to a crucifixion and death.

"Don't cling to me." Old securities and familiar ways are changed. And you and I know a thing or two about that. Enough books have been written to give chapter and verse for the strange newness of the times in which we are living. More changes, fundamental changes, have taken place in the world since I was born back in 1907 than in all the preceding centuries: nuclear fission, computers, medical knowledge, population growth, the rise of vast metropolitan areas, pollution, the mobility of families and people, an agricultural society transformed into an industrial and technological society— the list goes on and on. And with all this frightening change, no wonder we want to cling to the past in nostalgic longing for the good old simpler days. You and I can sing along with Archie and Edith Bunker, "Those were the days."

On the religious scene, it's no wonder that conservative churches and seminaries are booming and becoming more popular while the more liberal churches and seminaries theologically, are on the downgrade numerically. There is simply an overwhelming appeal in the face of the complexities of life today to return to the past, to the appeal of a simple gospel which takes the Bible simply and literally. I can understand the appeal. But the Easter story in John presents a different picture. "Don't cling to me." Don't cling to the old securities of the past. I will be smack in the middle of a new and radically different age for you, Mary. Don't hold on simply to what you have experienced in the past. There are new and wonderful things about to happen in the future.

The people of God have always had to learn that we can never sit down with God and say, this is the end, this is it. The time is fulfilled. Even the promised land was not the end for the people of God. Nor is the personal reassurance of Christ calling each of us by name on Easter morning. Like Abraham—and like Mary— we are called to pilgrimage with God in new and uncharted territory, with only his promise that he will be with us.

Mary accepted that. She accepted the new situation, scary as it must have been. She returned to the disciples and said, "I have seen the Lord." Trusting somehow— God knows how—that she would know that marvelous moment of recognition again: when he said to her, "Mary"—and the darkness was split in two and angels sang and bells rang and her whole world was flooded with light.

11.

Living with Humor

Harry N. Peelor

At the time he delivered The Protestant Hour *sermons, Harry N. Peelor was director of the Outreach Ministries Program of* Guideposts.

The year was 1977. James Earl Carter was inaugurated president of the United States. Pope Paul VI offered himself in exchange for eighty-six persons hijacked by German terrorists. David Berkowitz was arrested for the "Son of Sam" murders.

Many famous people died—comedian Freddie Prinze, Wernher Von Braun, Elvis Presley, Groucho Marx, Bing Crosby, and Charlie Chaplin.

Religion made news. Bishop John Neumann, known for developing the parochial school system, was canonized. The *New York Times* reported adverse reaction by religious leaders against the television series "Soap."

Movie theaters in 1977 were popping at the seams with people trying to get in to view a film titled *Oh God,* with the comedy star octogenarian George Burns as God and John Denver as his prophet.

A battered old man got up one night during a revival meeting and said, "Brothers and sisters, you know I haven't been what I ought to have been. I stole hogs, got drunk, told lies. I've been playing poker and gambling and I've been cussing and swearing, but through all of this, there's one thing I haven't done—I ain't never lost my religion."

If his religion was that of Jesus Christ, then what he was saying was sober truth. But I'll tell you something strange. There are people who have never stolen a hog, or been drunk, or got into fights, or gambled, or swore, or lied, but have lost their religion because they lost their sense of humor.

You have to have a sense of humor to be a Christian. You have to have a sense of humor to understand Jesus Christ and his revelation of God. Have you ever pictured Jesus laughing? If you never think of Jesus this way, you miss a lot in the Gospels—even if you read them faithfully.

In the most trying circumstances of life, there is still the potential for laughter. One of the reasons we may miss this dimension is a false, secular-sacred dichotomy. What happens in the church is sacred; what happens outside the church is secular. We try to separate life this way, but that's nonsense, for it is all one world.

Some people have come to the conclusion that if they were to think of Jesus with a sense of humor, they would be guilty of something blasphemous or sacrilegious. We do have preconceived notions of Jesus—the Man of Sorrows, the pale Galilean, meek and mild. Somehow when we think of Jesus, we confuse sincere and serious as if they meant the same thing. Many of us have a notion that to believe that Jesus would joke or laugh is somehow not quite right.

If we could lay aside some of our religious notions and read the Gospels again as if we were reading them for the first time, we might just find the joy and a Christ in whom we could delight. A strict, literal interpretation of the Bible misses so much of God's revelation. A strict, literal meaning of the Word misses the humor of Christ.

The literalism that misses the humor of Christ misses much more. It misses the point of what Jesus was saying and teaching. When Christ is presented as being constantly dour, solemn, and grim, he frankly becomes just plain dull. Hearts and minds that have been dulled by forced literalism need to open up again to the freshness and joy of Jesus.

Jesus used figures of speech. When he said, "I am the door," no one considered that he was saying that he was made of wood. He used figures of speech, which, pressed to the ultimate, would be ridiculous. We often become ridiculous in trying to twist, shape, and interpret literally what is meant figuratively.

In the book called *God in Everything,* Parson Jones writes to Miriam Gray:

> Many of the religious people I know talk of religion with a bedside manner and walk about in felt slippers. And if they speak of God, they tidy themselves first. But you go in and out of all the rooms in God's house as though you were quite at home. You open doors without knocking and you hum on the stairs, and it isn't always a hymn, either. My aunt thinks you are quite irreverent, but then, she can keep felt slippers on her mind without any trouble.

You'll never understand the humor of Jesus if you tiptoe through life with that kind of religion.

Let's take off our felt slippers and look at some of the warmth and humor of our Lord that emerges in the New Testament. One of the humorous devices he used was the preposterous statement. When we try to squeeze some literal truth out of these with deadly concentration and seriousness, the result is grotesque.

For example, most of us can recall the statement of our Lord that it is easier for a camel to go through the eye of a needle than for a rich man to get into the kingdom of heaven. Surely somewhere in your past, a pastor or Sunday school teacher has explained that the eye of a needle is the name of one of the gates of Jerusalem and that it is difficult for a camel to go through, but that if it gets down on its knees, it can be done. Our explanation is really funnier than what Jesus said. He was simply trying with this preposterous statement to wake up people to a sense of perspective and proportion about worldly goods. This camel was the same one he was talking about to the Pharisees when he said, "You wash the outside of the cup and you get it all polished and clean and you drink from it, but the inside is filthy. You strain out the gnats and then swallow the camel." It's the same camel. Can't you see it going down that long, stringy, Pharisaic neck—two humps and then the feet? It was funny, and it conveyed a truth that we mask with a grim, serious hunt for some other kind of worldly meaning.

What a wonderful Lord we have. How bad and sad it is that we block ourselves from the naturalness in his preposterous statements. He said, "Don't cast your pearls before swine." Nobody does, and that's the point of it all. He said to the disciples, "You will not always be well received in some towns. When you leave such a town, shake the dust off your feet." It's a surprise to me that there isn't a denomination now called "The Dust Shakers Off Their Feet," which has taken that little section seriously, and where, as part of the litany every Sunday morning, the people stand up and first shake one foot and then the other.

Jesus told a group of priests that it would be easier for harlots to get into heaven before them. The priests did not think it was very funny; it's a little bit like saying to preachers at a conference, "You know prostitutes are going to get into heaven before you preachers." It was a way of conveying truth that people, with their pompous, religious values and the love of their robes and ceremonial offices, needed to hear. Jesus just blasted these constrictions on life and dared them to open up with some freedom and love and warmth.

Sometimes the humor of Christ was not the rocking, deep laughter kind. Some of it simply evokes the smile that you just cannot resist when you run across something Jesus said that is so exact and right. It is the smile of self-recognition: "How did he know that about me? He is really right." We can accept and profit by lessons given this way. So Jesus told of the judge who would not listen to the widow's case until she wearied him with her persistence. If a mere man will listen finally because he is tired of being bothered, how much more can you count upon God being ever more ready to hear than we are to pray? I think that both the lesson and the way it was given are something to smile about.

Dr. Leslie Weatherhead, the famous British preacher, said the opposite of joy is not sorrow. The opposite of joy is unbelief. Jesus believed and so he could laugh. He can teach us to believe and to laugh again, if we will.

So much of the encounter of Jesus' life was with those who felt threatened by him—the political and religious authorities, the establishment. It's interesting to see how he waged his war with the establishment without being destructive, like some of those who think they fight the establishment now in his name. He said, "Do not think I have come to bring peace. I have come to bring a sword." Obviously, there were those who were thinking already of Jesus in terms of "gentle

Jesus, meek and mild," and he had to blast that picture. He did, but it was with that wry kind of statement that was never intended to authorize the use of force to destroy what we do not believe in. Apparently on that occasion even the disciples got trapped in literalism, for one of them said, "Lord, here are two swords." Jesus, in exasperation I am sure, said, "It is enough. All right, two swords will be enough."

So warm, so real, with the humor that isn't the kind of humor that is reaching out for another story to top the last one that was told, but a humor that comes swelling up naturally out of a complete and healthy life, a life of good cheer committed to making everyone else's life abundant—that is the kind of Lord we have. Of course he has a sense of humor. Of course he laughs.

When you read the words of Jesus in your Bible, "Do you expect to get grapes off thorns and figs off thistles?" you're not supposed to fold your hands in pious prayer and straighten your face and get a solemn countenance. It's all right to laugh.

Take a section of the Scripture with which you are familiar and where Jesus is speaking. Read the words, and then stop yourself in the middle of them and ask, "What picture do I have of Jesus now?"

I believe that most of us, if we are honest with ourselves, imagine that a great deal of the time when Jesus is speaking in the Scripture, he is shouting at us and he is very angry.

In our Scripture lesson, we find Jesus a guest in a home, and a man does not give him a towel to wipe the dust from his feet. Jesus points this out: "You gave me no towel to clean my feet, and this lady, whom you call a sinner, has washed my feet with perfumed tears and dried them with her hair." Do you think Jesus was screaming at that man when he said that? Don't you think there was something of a smile, and the way he conveyed this would always make a difference on the one who heard?

The use of irony was one of his weapons that got past the defenses of those who had a natural resistance to him. It made him winsome, interesting, and helped people to realize that he really did care. With irony, he rejected the bronze plaque type of philanthropy. He said, "When you give alms, sound no trumpet before you." How could we have missed the humor or the point of that advice? Then he gives it a further twist. "Such people," he said, "have their reward." It was another way of saying to us, "You be careful of what you ask of life, because you may just get it."

In another place, Jesus used the same irony in an even more unmistakable way in a warning to those who think religion is dull and deadly. As translated by J. B. Phillips, Jesus said, "Do not be dismal in the name of religion, or you will get your reward, you will be dismal."

Because Jesus starts with us just where we are, we can take off the veneer from the Scripture and our interpretation of our Lord, and encounter a whole, new Christ. His entire relationship with us may be much different from what we thought. We might, by simply remembering the dimension of the humor of Christ, find that we can really love him and delight in him as we have always wished.

For example, that terrible, embarrassing thing in your life or mine that we hope no one will find out about, and that we are so ashamed of—how do you picture Christ in relation to that? Do you see him standing somewhere in the wings, shaking his head and wagging his finger and saying to you, "Shame, shame"? What if it isn't like that at all? What if he is standing with a tear in his eye, because there is sorrow in the heart of God, but with a smile on his face as he moves toward you with warm laughter, putting his arms around you and forgiving you, restoring you and making you whole?

We do some funny things and then project them into the thinking of our Lord. For instance, imagine one of our teenagers out with the family car and getting in a little late some evening. There's that last 30 minutes, 45 minutes, and you begin to have visions of cars smashed, bodies flying and not discovered. You consider calling the local hospitals to see if there have been any admissions lately of somebody that age, and you wonder if you should call the police. You consider calling the parents of some of the other young people who were with your child. You go through all this with wringing of hands and growing anxiety, and then suddenly, there's that wonderful moment when the lights of the car are in the driveway, and your son or daughter is home.

As soon as the doors open, do we rush to a child, throw our arms around him, and say, "You're all right, thank God, you're all right"? We do not. We say, "Where have you been? What's the matter with you? Don't you know what I've been through?"

Is it not like that with the Lord of love and his relationship to the things that are wrong in your life, or mine? What if he doesn't deal with us in the same way we deal with our children? What if he can stand and see the stain of sin in our lives and still smile because he believes in the ultimate victory of righteousness? What if he can laugh at our evil because he's confident of the goodness and love in God that cannot be conquered? Don't you want to walk with that kind of a Lord?

Couldn't you make that kind of a Lord winsome enough so that somebody else could find him Savior, too?

This great Jesus with his sense of humor and perspective that keeps us from taking ourselves too seriously, or too lightly, helps us to discover ourselves, relax, and be ourselves.

When he saw Simon and Andrew fishing, he watched them for a while and then said, "Simon, Andrew, why don't you follow me? I will make you fishers of men." Don't you think they responded with a smile as well as with their lives? But we take that phrase, "fishers of men," and we put it on little pins, form clubs about it, write hymns about it, and make it so prim and so solemn that to belong to that kind of organization is totally different from what it's like to go fishing, so different that all of the joy is squeezed out of being a "fisher of men." Jesus doesn't want that.

He has the capacity to see inside the hearts of people. He knows that inside each of us there is a capacity to be loyal to the royal. So he could look at Peter who was a liar, and a coward, and a pretty good hindrance to the work of God. Jesus saw this vacillating human being and called him "the Rock." It's like calling a fat man Slim or tall man Shorty. A rock Peter was not—but a rock Peter became because Christ saw something deep within him and turned it loose.

A diary was found of a man who died during the First World War. Apparently, he had been writing in it the night he was killed. These are some of the words he wrote:

> The courage and good deeds of Jesus and his freedom
> from conventionality and puritanism, his rough, hard
> life, his direct simplicity and unswerving faith, his crisp,
> incisive judgment, and the keen satire with which he

crumbled the sophistries of the legal mind—all these things appeal to simple and plain folk who were sick to death of the eternal wranglings of their religious leaders about tradition and precedent. And they were responsible for the inclusion in the circle of Disciples of many a type which never before and since has felt welcome in religious society.

Each of us can experience that welcome and each of us can be that welcome. We can be in a whole new relationship with a Christ who has a sense of humor and who can laugh. And we can learn to laugh again and be the kind of people who will make it easier for others to be Christian.

Listen to the Scripture and the wry humor of Christ as he says to the people, "What in the world do you want? This generation is like some children in the marketplace. They complain that they pipe and you won't dance; they wail and you won't weep. John the Baptist came eating no bread and drinking no wine and you say that he is possessed by a demon. The Son of Man has come eating and drinking and you say, 'Behold, a glutton and a drunkard, a friend of tax collectors and sinners.'"

What do you want from this Christ? He seems willing to rest the case in the consequences of human lives in their relationship with him. I truly believe that it was trivial to our Lord that he was criticized by the pious people as being outrageously shocking. I am certain with some sense of humor, some deep laughter, he can promise you and me a relationship with him that will enrich our lives and the lives we touch. I think that is something that can spread a smile all through our being, and turn on in heaven the laughter of angels.

12.

Elijah: The Man Who Had the Blues

John A. Redhead, Jr.

At the time he delivered The Protestant Hour *sermons, John A. Redhead, Jr., was pastor of First Presbyterian Church in Greensboro, North Carolina.*

The year was 1964. In Vietnam, the Gulf of Tonkin Resolution was passed allowing the United States Navy to strike back, escalating the war. In China, an A-bomb was detonated. Back home, J. Edgar Hoover called Martin Luther King, Jr., "the most notorious liar in the country."

Martin Luther King, Jr., won the Nobel Peace Prize. Arnold Palmer won his fourth Masters tournament. At the Academy Awards, the movie *My Fair Lady* won best picture.

And Pope Paul VI visited Jerusalem, meeting with Jordan's King Hussein and the Orthodox Patriarch of Jerusalem.

It is enough; now, O Lord, take away my life.
(I Kings 19:4)

Many times you have heard people talk about being "under the weather." What they usually mean is that they are not feeling up to par physically. Being "under the weather" often gives you "the blues," that condition of the spirit which is as inelegant as the expression.

And one thing you can say about it is that in most people it is natural and can be expected. Just as the mercury rises and falls according to the temperatures of the weather; just as the surface of the earth is not level but rises at some points into mountains and falls away at others into valleys; just as the tides ebb and flow; so there are ups and downs in the weather and topography of the spirit. No one can expect to live always in the hills of thrills. It is only human that sometimes moods change and the road winds down into the valley.

For example, take a man like Elijah. When you think of him, you think of a man who was as strong as iron; but anyone who is familiar with his life knows that there came a time when he had the blues. The text tells us that he "came and sat down under a broom tree; and he asked that he might die, saying, 'It is enough; now, O Lord, take away my life.'"

You have felt that way too sometimes; and though you would like to know the cure, you wonder what it has to do with religion and by what right it is made the subject for a sermon. The answer is that the blues is just a name for low spirits, and anything which concerns the spirit concerns your faith. God knew what to do for Elijah to put him back on his feet, and when you read between the lines in this story you will find there a set of truths that has meaning for you.

I.

The first thing God did for Elijah was to tell him to look out for his physical well-being. The prophet had been through a severe physical and emotional experience and his resources were at a low ebb.

You remember the situation. When the Israelites moved into Palestine, they found there a native religion known as the worship of the Baals. Baal worship was a nature religion, whose object was to persuade the Almighty to grant production of crops and reproduction in animals; and its emphasis upon the sex motif went the length of providing temple prostitutes for licentious rites. For many years there was a running battle between the pagan religion and the true religion, and it came to a climax during the lifetime of Elijah. He gathered the 450 priests of Baal on Mount Carmel and challenged them to a test. The test was to see which deity, Jehovah or Baal, could send fire to burn the wood under a sacrifice. "You call on the name of your god," the prophet said to the priests, "and I will call on the name of the Lord; and the God who answers by fire, he is God." The priests of Baal tried and tried, but nothing happened; and then Elijah called on the name of the Lord and the fire fell and the sacrifice was consumed. And having won the test, he seized the 450 priests and put them to death.

Now a man named Ahab was king and his wife was Jezebel. She happened to be a worshiper of the Baals and when she heard what had happened she was hopping mad. She sent a messenger to Elijah and told him, "So may the gods do to me and more also, if I do not make your life as the life of one of them by this time tomorrow." Then Elijah was afraid, "and he arose and went for his life, and came to Beersheba." Then he went a day's journey into the wilderness and "came and sat down under a broom tree; and he asked that he might die, saying, 'It is enough; now, O Lord, take away my life.'"

Just put yourself in his place and see how you would feel. Suppose you had gone through that nerve-racking test on Mount Carmel: one man against 450, with all the tension of waiting for the result. Then no sooner is that over when you get word the queen is on your trail with the purpose of putting you to death. You don't stop to think of getting anything to eat, and you set off to put as many miles as possible between yourself and your pursuer. Is there any wonder that this man was utterly exhausted—physically, emotionally, nervously exhausted?

The trouble with him was that he was tired and hungry, and God, like the Good Physician that he is, said to him, The journey has been too great for you, lie down and sleep. So Elijah lay down and went to sleep, and when he awoke he found food and drink by his side. "Arise and eat," said God; and when he had eaten he lay down and slept again. The first thing God did for the man who had the blues was to look after his physical well-being.

The laws of health are the laws of God; and one of the most useful bits of God's truth you can get your hands on is this: You are compounded of body, mind, and spirit. These parts of your being are so closely tied together that the condition of one vitally affects the condition of the others. If the vitality of your physical being is at a low ebb, it is nothing to be wondered at that you are depressed in mind and spirit.

Dr. Louis Evans takes our truth and puts it like this: The parts of your being are so closely related that they catch each other's diseases. So take a cue from Elijah. When your husband mopes around the house, with the corners of his mouth set at twenty minutes after eight, and colors the whole atmosphere with indigo, give him a good lunch and send him out for a game of golf; the food and the exercise will work wonders. And then, when you need it yourself, have the good sense to make the same diagnosis and take the same prescription.

II.

That was the first thing God did for Elijah: He taught him to look out for his well-being. The second was this: He suggested that Elijah change his pattern of thinking.

The prophet had developed the bad habit of always looking on the dark side. Here was the king of Israel who had gone up to Tyre and had married a foreign queen, and she was the stronger personality of the two and she had wound him round her little finger and kept him under her thumb. More than that, she was a devotee of this pagan religion and had given the blessing of the royal house to the priests of Baal; and many of the people, not wishing to risk the disfavor of the queen, had deserted the worship of the true God. Elijah could think of nothing else. Listen to him: "Lord," he says, "the people of Israel have forsaken thy covenant, thrown down thy altars, and slain thy prophets with the sword; and I, even I only, am left."

And what did God do? He told Elijah to take his eyes off the dark spots in the picture and to form the habit of thinking about the plus instead of the minus. The royal house is in the hands of pagans, and that is bad. The true faith is suffering from the meddling of this idolatrous queen, and that is bad too. But look at the assets, Elijah. You are left to me, and you have shown yourself a stout ally in times past; as long as I have you I have a powerful leader, do I not? And not only do I have you, but I have others as well. "I will leave seven thousand in Israel, all the knees that have not bowed to Baal." And that number was symbolic, as is the number seven usually in the Bible. It adds the number four, which means completeness, to the divine number three, and it gets the perfect number seven. What God was saying to Elijah was that there were yet resources sufficient to turn the tide of paganism and save the nation for the true God; and the time had come for him to stop thinking so much about the difficulties and begin to look at what might be counted upon to yield dividends.

There is a useful truth here, and that is that sometimes the cause of our low spirits is not so much physical as mental. We think about the wrong things. We develop a habit of thought which majors on the minuses: And there is no one in such fortunate circumstances but that he can become a pessimist of the first order if he wishes to think only of his hard luck. You can take a little thing as small as a dime and hold it so close to your eye that it shuts out all light; and you can take your tough breaks and let them monopolize your thinking to the point of feeling so sorry for yourself you are ready to throw in the sponge.

If you wish to do so, you can always work yourself up a good case of the blues by counting your complaints. But if, first thing on waking every morning, you try to think of at least ten good things you are grateful for at the moment, then your facial clock will move from eight-twenty to ten-ten.

Dr. Wallace Hamilton has a story about a man who had lived on the same old farm all his life, who grew tired of it and wanted a change. Nothing about the place suited him, and at last he made up his mind he would sell it and buy another more to his liking. He listed the farm with a real estate broker, who at once prepared a sales advertisement for the newspaper; but before turning in the copy, he read over to the man the flattering description of the property which he had prepared. He talked of the farm's advantages: its ideal location, its up-to-date equipment, its fertile acres, its well-bred livestock. "Wait a minute," said the farmer; "read that again, and take it slow." So the salesman re-read the description. "Changed my mind," said the farmer. "I'm not going to sell. All my life I've been looking for a place just like that."

There is an old song that some of us used to sing in Sunday school and it had a refrain which went like this: "Count your many blessings, Name them one by one; And it will surprise you what the Lord has done." That is the second thing the prophet learned.

III.

Having brought Elijah's physical condition up to par and having given the right set to his mind, God does a third thing for him: He gives him something to do. "What are you doing here, Elijah?" He wasn't doing anything, but lying flat on his back feeling sorry for himself. And God gave him something to do. "Go, return on your way to the wilderness of Damascus," he said, and "anoint Hazael to be king over Syria; and Jehu . . . you shall anoint to be king over Israel; and Elisha the son of Shaphat . . . you shall anoint to be prophet in your place." God gave Elijah something to do and it made a new man of him.

You will notice that your pessimists are always the men and women who sit off on the sidelines in their comfortable arm chairs and write books about how fast the world is going to the dogs—like Arthur Schopenhauer and George Eliot and Bernard Shaw. But let them leave the sidelines and get in the game, and you have a William Booth with his Salvation Army, and a Jane Addams with her Hull House, and a Wilfred Grenfell with his mission to Labrador. That is what happened to Elijah. "Get up and get busy," God said to him; and once he went back to the firing line, you hear no more from him about the blues.

Here is a truth that will work just as well in the twentieth century A.D. as in the eighth century B.C., and what it says is this: If you get blue because you think your world is going to the dogs, then take hold of some part of it and see that it doesn't happen. If it be the problem of war which bothers you, then get in the game on the side of peace: Line up with a group like the World Federalists and work for world government based on law. If it is the ineffectiveness of your church which bothers you, get in the game: Go down there at ten o'clock on Sunday mornings and you will find plenty of young Elishas waiting to be taught. If you are concerned about the disintegration of the family, get hold of a conviction concerning the permanence of marriage and put a stop to this pagan propaganda that if a husband and wife do not have a feeling of affection any longer it is reason enough for separating. If you deplore the ravages of alcoholism, make up your mind that you know at least one person who is willing to practice voluntary abstinence. If you are concerned about the breakdown of moral standards among young people, you can be sure there is one parent in your town who knows where his sons and daughters are and what they are doing.

The Chinese have a proverb for it. They say: "It's better to light a candle than to curse the darkness." And the very act of lighting will drive away the darkness.

Here then is God's prescription that worked for his prophet. You can take it and interpret its meaning for yourself.